Lloyd George: The Man and His Story

by

Frank Dilnot

The Echo Library 2007

Published by

The Echo Library

Echo Library
131 High St.
Teddington
Middlesex TW11 8HH

www.echo-library.com

Please report serious faults in the text to complaints@echo-library.com

ISBN 978-1-40686-126-6

CONTENTS

FOREWORD

FOREWORD

Mr. Lloyd George gets a grip on those who read about him, but his personality is far more powerful and fascinating to those who have known the man himself, known him during the time his genius has been forcing him to eminence. He does not fill the eye as a sanctified hero should; he is too vitally human, too affectionate, too bitter, and he has, moreover, springs of humor which bubble up continually. (You cannot imagine an archangel with a sense of humor.) But it is this very mixture in the man that holds the character student. Lloyd George is quite unpretentious, loves children, will join heartily in the chorus of a popular song, and yet there is concealed behind these softer traits a stark and desperate courage which leads him always to the policy of make or break. He is flamingly sincere, and yet no subtler statesman ever walked the boards at Westminster. That is the man I have seen at close quarters for years. Is it to be wondered at that he alternately bewilders, attracts, and dominates high-browed intellectuals? Strangely enough, it is the common people who understand Lloyd George better than the clever ones. Explain that how you will.

I have seen David Lloyd George, present Prime Minister of England, as the young political free-lance fighting furiously for unpopular causes, fighting sometimes from sheer love of battle. I have seen him in that same period in moods of persuasion and appeal pleading the cause of the inarticulate masses of the poor with an intensity which has thrilled a placid British audience to the verge of tears. Since then I have seen him under the venomous attacks of aristocrats and plutocrats in Parliament when his eyes have sparkled as he has turned on them and hissed out to their faces words which burned and seared them and caused them to shake with passion. And in the midst of this orgy of hate which encircled him I have seen him in his home with his twelve-year-old blue-eyed daughter Megan curled up in his lap, his face brimming with merriment as, with her arm around his neck, she asserted her will in regard to school and holidays over a happy and indulgent father. That is the kind of man who now rules England, rules her with an absoluteness granted to no man, king or statesman, since the British became a nation. A reserved people like the British, conservative by instinct, with centuries of caste feeling behind them, have unreservedly and with acclamation placed their fate in the hands of one who began life as a village boy. It was but recently I was talking with a blacksmith hammering out horseshoes at Llanystumdwy in Wales who was a school-mate of Lloyd George in those days not so very long ago. The Prime Minister still has his home down there and talks to the blacksmith and to others of his school companions, for he and they are still one people together, with ties which it is impossible for statecraft to break—or to forge. I have met Lloyd George in private, have seen him among his own people at his Welsh home, and for five years as a journalist I had the opportunity of observing him from the gallery of the British Houses of Parliament, five years during which he introduced his famous Budget, forced a fight with the House of Lords, and broke their power. I purpose to tell in plain words the drama of the man as I have seen it.

A year before the war broke out, while he was still bitterly hated by the Conservatives, I was visiting him at his Welsh home near Llanystumdwy and he asked me what I thought of the district. I said it was all very beautiful, as indeed it was. I emphasized my appreciation by saying that the visitors at the big hotel at Criccieth near by were one and all enchanted. They were nearly all Conservatives, I pointed out, and there was just one fly in their ointment. "I know it," said Lloyd George, vivaciously, with a quick twinkle in his eye. "Here's a bay like the Bay of Naples, God's great mountains behind, beautiful woods, and green meadows, and trickling streams—everything the heart of man can desire, and in the midst of it all HE lives." He paused and deepened his voice. "Satan in the Garden of Eden," he said. It was just his twist of humor, but it told a story. Now for the companion picture. The last time I saw Lloyd George was one dark evening in the December which has just gone by. It had been a day of big political happenings; the Asquith Government had resigned, Bonar Law, the Conservative leader, had been asked by the King to form a Ministry and had said he could not do so. Lloyd George's name was being bandied about. In those few fateful hours Britain was without a Government. At seven o'clock I was at the entrance of the War Office at Whitehall. Through the dark street an automobile dashed up. The door was opened, and a silk-hatted man stepped out and passed rapidly into the War Office, and then the little group of bystanders noticed that the footman at the door of the automobile was wearing the royal livery. The silk-hatted visitor was obviously a messenger from King George. Three minutes later the War Office doors swung open and two men came hurrying out. The first was the King's messenger, the second was Lloyd George. The latter's shoulders were hunched with haste, his hat was pressed deep and irregularly over his forehead, his face, set hard, was canted forward. He almost scrambled into the conveyance, and three seconds later the automobile was going at top speed for Buckingham Palace. The King had sent for Lloyd George to ask him to become his Prime Minister.

F. D.

January, 1917.

I

THE VILLAGE COBBLER WHO HELPED THE BRITISH EMPIRE

One day in the year 1866 a middle-aged cobbler named Richard Lloyd, occupying a tiny cottage in the village of Llanystumdwy in North Wales, had a letter delivered to him by the postman which was to alter the whole of his simple and placid life. It was a letter from his sister and bore melancholy tidings. The letter told how she had lost her husband and how she and her two little children were in distress. She was the mother of the present Prime Minister of Britain. The elder of her two children, then three years old, was David Lloyd George.

Miss Lloyd, the sister of Richard Lloyd, the cobbler, had married, a few years before, a William George who came of farming people in South Wales. A studious young fellow, he had devoted himself to reading, and presently passed the examinations necessary to become a teacher in the elementary schools. The countryside offered him no opportunity of advancement and he migrated to the big city of Manchester, where he secured a position as master in one of the national schools of the district. In Manchester were born two children, the elder of whom, David, was fated in after years to rise to fame. David's birthday was January 17, 1863. Far indeed were thoughts of future eminence from the struggling family during that time in Manchester.

Under the strain of city life the health of William George began to fail. Country-bred as he was, he pined for the open air of the fields and the valleys, and very soon the doctor gave him no choice and told him that if he wished to prolong his life he must leave the city streets. And so it came about that William George and the two children forsook Manchester and went back again to country life in South Wales to a place called Haverfordwest. William George took a farm and for a year or more he and his wife toiled on it. How much of the work fell on Mrs. George can only be guessed, but she must have carried a full share, for her husband's health was undermined, and the home had to be kept up not only for the sake of her husband, but the children as well. She was in delicate health, and her efforts must have been arduous and painful. Withal, destiny had its severest blow still in hand. William George had not recovered his strength; an attack of pneumonia came upon him, and his death occurred some few months after leaving Manchester.

Mrs. George, overwhelmed by the death of her husband, was at the same time faced by financial difficulties and the problem of maintaining the existence of herself and her two children. To carry on the farm single-handed was impossible. There were, moreover, immediate liabilities to be met. She could find no way out, and the upshot was a public auction sale of the farm effects and the household furniture. Three-year-old David, not understanding the tragedy of it all, was nevertheless impressed by the scene on the day the neighbors came to bid for, and to buy, the things that made up his mother's home. Even now he can recall how the tables and chairs from the house, and the plows and harrows from the fields, were scheduled and ticketed in and around the homestead and disposed of by the auction to the highest bidder. He could not understand it, but somewhere deep within the sensitive child was struck a note of pain, the echoes of which have never left him throughout his strenuous life. He felt dimly in his childlike way the loneliness of his mother. He has never forgotten it. Lonely indeed she was. She had but one friend to turn to, and that one friend was her brother, Richard Lloyd, the village shoemaker up in North Wales. To him she wrote and told her story.

It was her letter which Richard Lloyd paused in his work to read that day some fifty years ago. This village cobbler, destined unwittingly to play such an important part in the history of the British Empire, is still alive and hale and hearty, still lives in his old district. I saw him recently, a tall, erect, fearless-eyed man, though in the neighborhood of ninety, perhaps past that age. He had a full beard, snow-white, and a clean-shaven upper lip, reminiscent of the fashion of half a century ago. He lives, of course, in comfort now and enjoys a dignified, happy old age. Vigorous still, he continues to preach in the chapel of the Nonconformist denomination of which he is a member. I tried to picture him as he must have been fifty years back, a studious, middle-aged man, rigidly religious, a confirmed bachelor, dividing his time between his calling, on the one hand, and the study of the Bible, on the other.

He lived at that time a laborious life, frugal by necessity, doing his duty as he saw it, and I dare say he appeared to a casual observer an uninteresting village type, a silent man, sincere in his bigoted way, but colorless as such persons must always be to those of a different class. To me he will remain one of the most interesting men I have ever seen. Richard Lloyd read his sister's letter and formed his resolution. He decided to go to her help. And thus it was he journeyed to South Wales and brought the widow and her two little boys up north to Llanystumdwy, where he lived. He installed them in his cottage, a little two-story residence with a tiny workshop abutting from it at the side where he carried on his shoe-mending. In front the main road ran by, twisting its way through the village, and thence through woods and meadows, and giving access within a mile on either side to park-lands attached to the big country houses of wealthy people to whom the village cobbler was a nonentity and a person of a different order of beings from themselves. They were not to know, these rich neighbors, that the cobbler was bringing for protection to his humble home a child destined to be a Prime Minister of the country. Prime Minister in a crisis of its history.

Of the little family's years of struggle there are a few glimpses. Cheerfully Richard Lloyd bent himself to his self-imposed task of lightening his sister's lot, and Mrs. George worked hard that her children should not suffer from want. There was no money to spare in the household. Mrs. George baked bread so as not to take anything from their small resources for the baker. Twice a week there was a little meat for the family. Subsequently, as the children grew bigger, a tiny luxury was here and there found for them. At Sunday morning breakfast, for example, they received as a treat half an egg each to eat with their bread-and-butter. In the garden behind the cottage vegetables were grown to eke out supplies, and it was one of the tasks of young Lloyd George to dig up the potatoes for the household.

Llanystumdwy, the boyhood home of Lloyd George, is a picturesque village, a mile or so from the sea, nestling at the foot of the Snowdon range. Meadows and woods embower Llanystumdwy. Rushing through the village a rock-strewn stream pours down from the mountains to the sea, with the trees on its banks locking their branches overhead in an irregular green archway. Look westward to the coast from Llanystumdwy and you have in Carnavon Bay one of the finest seascapes in Britain. Turn to the east, and the rising mountains culminate in the white summit of Snowdon and other giant peaks stretching upward through the clouds. Could Providence have selected a more fitting spot for the upgrowth of a romantic boy? Lloyd George's Celtic heart had an environment made for it in this nook between the Welsh mountains and the sea. Little wonder that he has never left the place. At the present time his country house is on the slope overlooking Criccieth, about a mile from the old cobbler's cottage where he spent his boyhood forty years ago.

Lloyd George was sent quite early to the church elementary school with the other village children. There seems to have been nothing of the copy-book order about his behavior, nor are any moral lessons for the young to be drawn from it. He set no specially good example, was not particularly studious, was quite as mischievous if not more so than his schoolmates, and on top of all this—sad to relate after such a record—was practically always at the head of his class. He achieved without effort what others sought to accomplish by hard and persistent work. He just soaked up knowledge as a sponge soaks up water; he could not help it. Out of school hours he was a daring youngster filled with high spirits, and very active. He had dark-blue eyes, blackish hair, a delicate skin, and regular features, and the audacity within him was concealed behind a thoughtful, studious expression—just such a boy as a mother worships. That old Puritan, his uncle, worshiped him, too, though I am quite sure he concealed the fact behind the gravest and sometimes the most reproving of demeanors. An interesting point is that the vivacious and keen-witted child understood and was devoted to this serious-minded uncle of his. Richard Lloyd worked hard to make the boy grow up a straight-living, brave, and God-fearing man, and his influence on his young nephew was strong from the start. There is a story told about this. The children of the village school (which was connected with the Established Church of England) on each Ash Wednesday had to march from the school to the church, and were there made to give the responses to the Church Catechism and to recite the Apostles' Creed. That sturdy Nonconformist, Richard Lloyd, denied the right of the Church of England to force children, many of them belonging to Nonconformist parents, to go to church to subscribe to the Church doctrine. Lloyd George carefully digested his uncle's protest, and went away and organized a revolt among the children. The next time they went to church they refused to make the responses. Lloyd George as the ring-leader was punished, but the rebellion he organized stopped the practice of forcing Church dogmas into the mouths of the children. This is a very suggestive story. I know the main facts to be true because not so very long ago Lloyd George himself confirmed them to me. At the same time I beg leave to doubt whether any great spiritual fervor was the motive power of Master Lloyd George at that time. It was just the first outbreak of his desire for revolt against the powers that be—wicked powers because his uncle had said so—and the satisfaction of that instinct for audacious action which has marked him ever since. To me there was not much of the saint about the boy Lloyd George; he was just a young daredevil—which, on the whole, is perhaps the more attractive.

By the time Lloyd George was ten or eleven years of age his mother and his uncle became filled with thoughts as to his future. They both knew the boy was specially gifted, both realized that unless special effort were made he must inevitably drift from school into the lower ranks of labor, probably that of work on a farm. There were long and anxious consultations between the cobbler and his sister. Finally Richard Lloyd came to a decision, a decision which was to have a lasting effect on the destinies of the British nation. He resolved on a noble act, the nobler in that he had no idea what tremendous consequences would spring from it.

By long years of work and self-denial he had saved a little sum toward his old age. It amounted to a few hundred pounds. It was all he had. He decided to devote that sum toward the making of his nephew, Lloyd George, an educated man, toward putting him in a profession where he might have a chance in the world.

After the great speculation had been decided on it was settled that young David should be brought up as a solicitor. This necessitated not only the provision of certain heavy fees in connection with the examinations, but also time spent in a prolonged course of study. The few hundreds of pounds was a small-enough amount, and it was obvious that it would have to be sparingly expended if it were to cover all that was required. Young Lloyd George was a brilliant youth, but even his brilliancy could not help beyond a certain point. The old cobbler saw one way of economizing. He set himself the task of personally learning the elements of French and Latin in order to impart them to his nephew. I have often imagined the mental agony of the cobbler struggling with those foreign grammars. But he succeeded. His nephew also succeeded. Young George passed his preliminary examination and his intermediate without difficulty. Then while he progressed further he had to have experience in a solicitor's office—which ran away with more money. At twenty-one, however, he was finished, and was admitted a solicitor. All that had been gone through for him to reach this goal is shown by the fact that, having been formally enrolled as a lawyer, he and his family at that time could not raise the three guineas necessary to purchase the official robe without which he could not practise in the local courts. He at once went out and worked in an office and earned that three guineas.

He was now launched in the world. The great adventure of life began almost immediately for him.

II

HOW LLOYD GEORGE BECAME FAMOUS AT TWENTY-FIVE

The personalities of history flash across our vision like shooting-stars in the sky, emerging from hidden origins, making for their unknown goal with a speed and brilliance at once spectacular and mysterious. They are incalculable forces; we can only look at them and wonder at them. It is futile and quite useless to try to define the secret motive power of these personalities by puny analyses of moral influences and by a catalogue of their feelings and surroundings. They follow their destined course and raise our admiration or our fears and all the while they give us no real clue to the powers within their souls or the end they serve.

There had been many endeavors to link up Lloyd George with certain sets of beliefs; sincere persons have associated his prominence with his Liberalism, with his Nonconformity, with his passion for the interests of the poor, and in these later days with his fervor for national and patriotic effort. As a matter of fact, the framing of his dogmas has had little or nothing to do with the power of the man. He is one of those persons whom nature has made of dynamite; who would have blasted a way for himself in any kind of conditions. It is neither to his credit nor to his discredit that Heaven has given him an individuality which has taken him throughout life to distinction and high achievement. He has always swung to his tasks like a needle to the Pole.

It so happened that by the surroundings of his youth—the piety and pride and modest circumstances of his uncle and his mother—he was early thrown into certain spheres of activity. But these spheres were merely the medium for his powers. A wider survey than that of the enthusiastic Nonconformist or the patriotic Welshman shows that Lloyd George's nature would have cleaved its way like a sword through any obstacle in any cause. He simply could not have helped it. Destiny had set a mark on him from birth.

He was only seventeen when on a visit to London he went for the first time to the House of Commons to listen to the proceedings from the gallery and here is an abstract from his diary at that period: "Went to Houses of Parliament. Very much disappointed with them.... I will not say I eyed the assembly in the spirit in which William the Conqueror eyed England on his visit to Edward the Confessor—as the region of his future domain. O Vanity!" A country youth without money, without prospects, sitting in the exclusive Parliament House of the most exclusive nation of the world, watched the assembly before him and there occurred to him the thought of conquering it single-handed. That is what it came to. Of course his reference is in the nature of a joke. It could hardly be otherwise. But it was a joke which has proved to be a prophecy.

Before he was seventeen Lloyd George had already dived deep into controversy. His school of debating consisted of the cobbler's workshop and the village smithy at Llanystumdwy, where in the evenings young men and old men and a sprinkling of boys used to assemble to discuss in a haphazard way questions of ethics, the politics of the day, and most of all the rights and wrongs of the religious sects to which they respectively belonged. Richard Lloyd, on the one hand, and the old blacksmith, on the other, would stir the discussion now and again with a sagacious word. It is easy to imagine the ripple of musical Welsh which sometimes drowned the tap-tap of the cobbler's hammer, or was submerged beneath the clang of the anvil. The bright eyes and excited faces of these Celts partly illumined by the oil-lamp or by the sudden glow of the blacksmith's furnace must have provided pictures worth record for themselves, quite apart from the personal interest they would now possess.

In the midst of the discussions young David would plunge with a wit and understanding beyond his years, and he stood up to his seniors with both gravity and audacity. "Do you know," said the gray-haired blacksmith to Richard Lloyd one day, "I really had to turn my serious attention to David last evening or he would have got the best of me."

If any of those who read this narrative are beginning to have an idea that this fourteen-year-old boy was by way of becoming a prig they may be relieved by the knowledge that when the youngster was not taking a hand in polemics in the smithy or the cobbler's cottage he was often enough leading the boys of the village into some kind of mischief. One old inhabitant came to have the fixed belief that David was the origin of pretty well all the mishaps in Llanystumdwy. Let a gate be found lifted from its hinges, a fence or hedge broken down, or windows smashed, and the old man had the one explanation, "It's that David Lloyd at it again."

It is important to know that Richard Lloyd, the shoemaker, was not only studious and intelligent, but was independent beyond his class. A kind of benevolent feudalism still existed in the district, and villagers at election time fell naturally into the groove required by the rich landowners and gentlefolk of the neighborhood. Once at an election three or four of the cottagers voted Liberal instead of Conservative. They were promptly turned out of their dwellings. The time came when the shoemaker was the only Liberal voter in the place. He remained quite unshaken by persuasion, influence, or material considerations. Lloyd George even as a young boy gloried in his stalwart uncle. He was rebellious that it should be possible to cow other people, and the knowledge of the prevalent thraldom poured deep into young Lloyd George's soul. This simple religious village folk lived hard, with but a week's wages between them and want, lived, so to speak, on sufferance under the vicar and squire and land-owner, who, while often kindly enough and even generous in their way, expected obedience, and who exacted servitude in all matters of opinion. The big people and the cottage folk were two entirely different sets of beings. What a precipice there was between them can hardly be understood by those who have not passed some time in the village life of Britain. A man who took a rabbit or hare from the preserved coverts of game extending for miles in all directions was rigorously prosecuted as a criminal. A man who took fish from prohibited waters was often a good deal more harshly adjudged than the drunken brute who beat his wife or the assailant in some desperate fight. And let it be noted that these superior people had veritable power of government, for from them were drawn the benches of magistrates—amateur local judges, who sat weekly or monthly, as the case might be, to punish evil-doers of the district. Many of these people in some of the relations of life were quite admirable, but when it came to any question of the protection of privilege, the preservation of property, or the rights in general of their superior class, these landowners were as merciless in the North Wales district as in many other parts of the country. Scorn and rage grew in the heart of young Lloyd George as he realized that these individuals had no claim over their fellows in personal worth or understanding, that they were practically unassailable by reason of their ramparts of wealth, that they lived in comfort, if not in luxury, while those whom they dominated were struggling hard for a bare subsistence. I can imagine the youth reciting the couplet which sets out the position:

God bless the squire and his relations,
And keep us in our proper stations.

Worldly knowledge and bookish knowledge were acquired by Lloyd George during the next few years while he was going through his law course in the office of a firm of solicitors in the neighboring little town of Portmadoc. While there he had further opportunity for developing his natural powers of oratory, for he became a member of a local debating society which regularly had set battles on all kinds of topics—political, literary, and social. At twenty-one his preliminaries ended and he became an admitted solicitor competent to practise law and to appear as an advocate in the local civil and criminal courts. He was penniless, he had no friends likely to help him in his profession. But he had confidence in himself. Hidden fires were burning behind those steady dark-blue eyes of his. The office work which he undertook to secure the money to buy his official robe was accomplished with a run. Then he put up a little brass plate announcing to all and sundry in the locality that he was prepared to practise law. Though he had no rich friends, he possessed certain assets in the reputation he had made among the residents of the district by his sparkling good humor, his ready sympathy with distress, and his vivacious wit in debate. Individuals of the humbler class soon began to come to the young solicitor for advice and assistance. He found himself engaged to defend people charged with small offenses before the local magistrates and to fight cases connected with small money transactions before the county court—which was the civil tribunal. Clients found in the young fellow not only a shrewd lawyer, but a friend who entered into their cases with ardor.

He differed from other lawyers of the country towns, men who had grown prosperous in their profession, in so far as he always put up a tremendous fight, whatever the chances of success. He was, moreover, never hampered by deference for the bench. It was the practice of the magistrates, most of them local land-owners and all of them belonging to the propertied classes, to browbeat any local solicitors who showed signs of presumption—that is to say, of independence and lack of what was regarded as proper respect in their conduct of cases before the court. Lloyd George said things and did things which the most experienced and successful solicitors of the district would have shrunk from as ruinous to their business. He made it a practice never to waste a word in any subservience to magistrates who showed an overbearing disposition. The magistrates, to their amazement, found they could not overawe the young upstart. When one realizes the unchallenged caste rule of those local bigwigs and the extraordinary respect which was paid to them by advocates and litigants alike, it is easy to understand the amazement and the shock which came upon them when young Lloyd George not only refused to submit to their bullying, but stood up to them and even thrust wounding words at them. It was an unheard-of proceeding. Some of these magistrates, lifelong supporters of Church and state, must sometimes have wondered why the presumptuous youth was not struck dead by Providence for his temerity. He, on his part, was never so happy as when he was shocking them. Clients quickly grew in number. The farmers found him an enthusiastic defender of their rights, the shopkeepers trusted him with their small business worries, and if there were any poachers to be defended where was there to be found so able, so sympathetic, and so fearless an advocate as young Lloyd George? All this time it must be remembered he was but early in the twenties, little more than a boy.

Many instances might be given of his audacity in the face of the lordly magistrates before whom he appeared. Here is one that is typical. Lloyd George was retained to defend four men who were charged with illegally taking fish from prohibited waters—in other words, accused of poaching, the most deadly sin of all to the owners of the land. The case was tried before a big bench of magistrates, all of them local celebrities. Early in the proceedings Lloyd George put in a plea that the court had no jurisdiction in the matter. In response the chairman—the presiding magistrate—replied grandiloquently that such a point must be decided by a higher court.

"Yes, sir," said Lloyd George, "and in a perfectly just and unbiased court."

The magistrate stared open-eyed at this impudence, and promptly proceeded to put Lloyd George in his place. "If," said he, "that remark is intended as a reflection on any magistrate sitting on this bench I hope Mr. George will name him. A more insulting and ungentlemanly remark to the bench I have never heard during my experience as a magistrate."

"Yes," replied Lloyd George, "and a more true remark was never made in any court of justice."

This was more than flesh and blood could stand. In admonitory tone the chairman said: "Tell me to whom you are referring. I must insist upon your stating if you are referring to any magistrate sitting in this court."

"I refer to you in particular, sir," said Lloyd George.

"Then I retire from the bench," said the chairman, rising from his place. He turned to his fellow-magistrates. "This is the first time I have ever been insulted in a court of justice."

14

In company with a colleague he left the court. A third magistrate remarked that he could not proceed with the case until Lloyd George had apologized.

"I am glad to hear it," said Lloyd George, imperturbably. Promptly another magistrate went out. One of the few justices remaining repeated the demand for an apology. Instead of apologizing Lloyd George made the following reply; "I say this, that at least two or three magistrates of this court are bent upon securing a conviction whether there is a fair case or not. I am sorry the chairman left the court, because I am in a position to prove what I have said. I shall not withdraw anything, because every word I have spoken is true."

This was really too much. All the lot of the magistrates went out, their departure being accompanied by the few barbed words from the young advocate. What happened when the magistrates got together outside the courtroom can only be guessed. They must have had a painful discussion among themselves, because presently four of them came in and rather meekly said they would try the case, though they again made a protest to the effect that Lloyd George really ought to apologize. Of course he did not do so.

It was when Lloyd George was twenty-five and was already a highly popular figure throughout a large part of Wales that he sprang suddenly into a wider notice and may be said to have had for the first time the eyes of the whole country centered on him. Wales is a country of Nonconformists who attend religious services in their own chapels and do not—at least the great majority of them—belong to the Established Church of England. The state Church, however, is implanted throughout the country, and it is only to be expected that local friction should sometimes arise.

In a village at the foot of Snowdon an old quarryman died, and before he passed away expressed the wish that he should be laid by the side of his daughter, who was buried in the graveyard of the Church of England. The Church clergyman would not consent to the Nonconformist rites being performed if the old man were buried where he desired to be. The old man, he said, could not be placed by the side of his daughter, but must be buried in a remote portion of the graveyard reserved for unknown people and for suicides. The Nonconformists of the village were outraged at the suggestion. They went to young Lloyd George and asked his advice about the matter. Lloyd George plunged deep into legal enactments, into the local conditions, and all the facts pertaining to the case. Then he delivered a characteristic judgment. "You have the right," he said, "to bury this man by the side of his daughter in the churchyard. If the clergyman refuses you permission proceed with the body to the graveyard. Take the coffin in by force, if necessary. If the churchyard gates are locked against you, break them down." The villagers faithfully followed the suggestion of the young lawyer. They took the body to the churchyard—I believe Lloyd George accompanied them—and they broke down the locked churchyard gates, dug a grave for the old man by the side of his daughter, and buried him there. The Church authorities were scandalized and an action at law was the result. It was heard in the local county court before a judge and jury. Lloyd George defended the villagers, and the jury, influenced by his speech, returned a verdict in their favor. The judge, however, said that Lloyd George was wrong on a point of law and decided the case on the side of the Church. Lloyd George instantly said that the matter could not rest, and on behalf of the villagers he appealed against the decision to the Lord Chief Justice in London. The case was heard by the Lord Chief and another judge, and they came to the conclusion that the jury's decision was right, that the county-court judge was wrong, and that Lloyd George was perfectly correct on the point of law in connection with which he had been overruled.

Lloyd George was twenty-five when he secured this triumph. All the public were interested in the case, and in the Welsh townships and villages his name flamed out like a beacon.

III

FIGHTING THE LONE HAND

Lloyd George was twenty-five when his fight for the burial of the old quarryman lifted him to the public notice of the country at large. The year was a fateful one for him in other respects. For two or three years before this he had been speaking at public meetings, securing more and more confidence as he realized his powers. He became the banner-bearer for the allied causes of democracy, a free Church, and the rights of Wales as a nation. His compatriots rallied round him as their forefathers had rallied round Owen Glendower centuries before.

Working early and late, Lloyd George united his professional engagements with appearances on the public platform. He was already rousing those eddies of hatred and that personal devotion on which he has been borne to fame. Furiously he flung himself into attacks on the classes from which his political opponents were drawn. He adopted new methods, he heeded not convention, made always for the thickest of the fray. All the time there was mixed with his fervor an element of shrewdness. It was this shrewdness, for instance, which sent him to a big gathering of his political opponents, where he sat quietly in a back seat in order to learn what they had to say about him, and listened to their abuse with keen satisfaction. Gleams of ambition must have been shooting in upon him by this time. It was impossible that he had not thoughts of a bigger future for himself, and yet it came as a thunderclap to him when he heard that he, a youthful free-lance, had been adopted by the Liberal associations of the district to be their candidate for Parliament at the next election. It may be imagined with what zest under this stimulation he carried on his preparations for the contest whenever it should arise. The constituency—Carnarvon Boroughs— comprised a group of towns and a large number of villages. It included castles and mansions and great estates; a considerable portion of the general body voters were associated with the landowners and aristocrats. Lloyd George must have felt it was a pretty hopeless fight, but a fight, nevertheless, which he would enjoy.

There is one other event to chronicle during this year when he reached the age of twenty-five. Upon the mountain slopes beyond Llanystumdwy was a spacious old farm-house, the home of a sweetly pretty Welsh girl named Maggie Owen. How or when Lloyd George first met her is not recorded, but in the course of his diary we come across a significant entry just before this time. The diary refers to a meeting of a debating society in which he had taken part, and goes on to relate "Took Maggie Owen home." It is hard to imagine young Lloyd George anything but an impetuous lover. His suit progressed, and in this same fateful year of 1888 he was married. It may be said in passing that never was a happier union, and that in the hard and adventurous life that lay before the young politician he found in Mrs. George a true companion. Marriage seemed to strengthen his ambition, and his vision began to spread over the general field of politics instead of remaining exclusively, as hitherto, fixed upon projects of special, if not of exclusive, interest to Wales. Nevertheless he continued the leading figure in the fight for reforms in his native country. A good deal of his enthusiasm, for example, was expended on Church disestablishment in Wales— that is to say, the separation of the English Church from state support and state endowment, in view of the fact that the majority of the people were Nonconformists, and that it was unfair to impose upon them an unwanted and costly church which they had to help support even though they were Nonconformist enthusiasts. There is nothing like a religious controversy to stir feelings strongly, and the conflicts in the campaign for disestablishment were very bitter. Lloyd George's chief opponent on the other side was the Bishop of St. Asaph, a prelate of the Church of England, himself a Welshman and a very able man. He gave the promoters of disestablishment some hard knocks, and it is related of him that he was particularly effective in one of the districts. Accordingly, the Nonconformists there brought down Lloyd George to speak at a public meeting in order to counteract the bishop's influence. Lloyd George himself tells the story of how he was introduced at that meeting by the chairman, a leading deacon of the village. "We have suffered much of late from misrepresentations," he said. "The Bishop of St. Asaph has been speaking against us and we all know that he is a very great liar. Thank God we have a match for him here to-night in Mr. Lloyd George." In later years when Lloyd George and the bishop became good friends in spite of their differences of opinion, it was hard to decide which of them enjoyed this story most.

Lloyd George began to speak everywhere, at street corners, in conventicles, in the market-places, at mass-meetings in the public buildings, and his peculiar oratory secured him larger and larger audiences and aroused attention, sympathetic or hostile, all over the constituency. Many who were lukewarm and went to hear him out of curiosity were swung by his personality into being supporters. He had always his own natural style of talk. Possessing a musical and clear voice, he never strained for effect, rarely used a rotund sentence, but talked to his audiences in a red-hot conversational kind of way, his heightened feelings finding expression in a sibilance which always touched the nerves of his hearers. He seldom interrupted interrupters, finding it more effective to let them speak and then to deal with them in his own special manner when they had finished. There were occasionally exceptions to this, however. In the course of one of his speeches he exclaimed, "What do my opponents really want?" A husky, hostile voice from the crowd broke in, "What I want is a change of government." "No," said Lloyd George; "what you really want is a change of drink." Another time he had begun a sentence with the words "I am here," when an opponent in the crowd shouted, "So am I." "Yes," said Lloyd George, "but you are not all there." One of his best retorts in his early days was to a Conservative who came to a Liberal meeting determined to stand no nonsense. "We must give home rule," declared Lloyd George, "not only to Ireland, but to Scotland as well, and to Wales." "And home rule for hell," shouted a man in the audience. "Quite right," said Lloyd George; "let every person stick up for his own country."

A hard-working young professional man, Lloyd George was in for a heavy fight and, in the opinion of many, a hopeless fight, when the election came two years later. It was a dramatic chance that selected for his Conservative opponent the squire of his native village, the dignitary to whom Lloyd George as a village lad used to touch his hat. Fierce excitement ranged throughout the election fight. In the result Lloyd George snatched victory by just a handful of votes, his poll being one thousand nine hundred sixty-three against the Conservative total of one thousand nine hundred forty-five. Lloyd George was twenty-seven at the time of this triumph and became known as "the boy politician." There were many sneers among his opponents, who pointed out that this fluent young demagogue had now reached the end of his tether. In the environment of the House of Commons, among really clever men, he would sink to the natural inconsequence from which a series of fortunate accidents had lifted him. And indeed it was not unnatural for even the sympathetic observer to feel that perhaps this was the end of Lloyd George, that the ability which he undoubtedly possessed and which had carried him a considerable distance was not the ability which could do any more for him. He had projected himself out of the congenial surroundings wherein his talents had proved of avail, but, like a spent rocket, he would now rapidly come to earth.

It would have been inconceivable to many of his friends and to all of his opponents that this twenty-seven-year-old M. P. should have regarded himself as but on the threshold of his work, should have looked upon what he had achieved merely as preliminaries to his rarely serious efforts in life. They would have smiled indulgently or ironically if they had been told at this period the story of Lloyd George's diary entry after his first visit to the House of Commons at seventeen. Probably no person on earth but his wife knew the steely determination behind her husband's impetuosity.

The young M.P. took his seat in the House of Commons on April 17, 1890. A Liberal Government was in power. Gladstone, over eighty years of age, was at the head of it. Political giants whose reputation had reached young Lloyd George through the newspapers were scattered along the two front benches. He sat himself down on one of the back seats and proceeded to look at these men in action and to weigh them up. He formed some judgments about them. Here is what he wrote about Mr. Asquith in the course of some work for a Welsh newspaper a little later on: "A short, thick-set, rather round-shouldered man with a face as clean shaven as that of the most advanced curate, keen eyes and a broad, intellectual forehead—he speaks clearly and emphatically. He sets out his arguments with great brilliancy and force." Little did the young M. P. think that in the years to come he would be supplanting this man as Prime Minister of the country.

Right from the start Lloyd George set himself to acquire the methods and fashions of the House of Commons, with all the involved procedure. He wanted to avoid the obvious pitfalls. Presently he essayed a speech, and though he confessed himself as nervous, he did well, and members spoke highly of his first effort. It is as well to say here that the House of Commons quickly cuts short the ambitions and hopes of many young men who on the strength of platform popularity look for triumph at Westminster. The House of Commons, whatever may be its drawbacks, has some human qualities, is kindly to beginners, has a respect for sincerity, an undisguised yawn for bores, and a cold contempt for swollen-headed young members who try to impress it with their capacity. When once a member has passed the stage of initial forbearance due to a new-comer, there grows upon him the fact that the House of Commons is indeed the most critical assembly in the world. There are always within it many who have secured their places by money or influence, but they are in the minority, and the House, as a whole, including even these rich men, has never any respect for moneyed men as such, pays no special deference to the person of lordly birth within its walls. A member is judged absolutely on what he is himself. The two most popular and respected members in the strangely mixed House of Commons I watched for years were Mr. Thomas Burt, the father of the House, who had been a working miner, and that ardent and lovable Irish Nationalist, Mr. Willie Redmond—both men having secured in extraordinary measure the personal affection of the whole House. In some respects, therefore, the House is like a big public school, and Conservatives and Liberals, notwithstanding their political differences, are welded together by a common instinct so far as the domestic character of the Chamber is concerned.

The peculiar atmosphere was not lost upon Lloyd George, and he diligently attuned himself to the new medium. This would have been unavailing if there had been nothing in his speeches, but it was soon realized that here was an interesting new member, a man inexperienced in some directions, but with bold thoughts, apt phrases, and an almost unpleasant sincerity. He did not take the House by storm, but still he was listened to. He quickly developed. Within a year his name was frequently in the newspapers as one of the guerrilla fighters below the gangway who gave the Government no peace.

Lloyd George had made up his mind about the statesmen in the House and had come to a decision that not even the strongest of them was unassailable. Gladstone led the Government and Lloyd George was his nominal follower, but on individual matters the young M. P. opposed his chief. It was rather like a fox-terrier standing up to a lion. Gladstone had an incomparable prestige, the result of a continuous half-century of work for his country, including four periods as Prime Minister. Probably three-quarters of the six hundred and seventy members of the House of Commons, many of them old politicians, would have been nervous about tackling Gladstone, who, despite his eighty years, was still a terrific force in debate, possessing an eagle mien which subdued opponent and recalcitrant supporters alike. Young Lloyd George refused to be cowed even by Gladstone.

Wales was pressing for the disestablishment of the English Church within its borders, and Lloyd George with two or three other Liberal members bitterly protested about the postponement of this reform. Difficulties of immediate parliamentary action, the urgency of other legislation, the opposition from powerful sections of the House, all these things were nothing to Lloyd George;

what he wanted was the disestablishment of the Church in Wales. Frequently the Prime Minister in the British Parliament ignores the attacks of the lesser men. Gladstone could not ignore Lloyd George. He had to answer him. Sometimes he condescended to berate him, much to the enjoyment of the assembly. Lloyd George always came up unhurt, alert, and persistent.

In 1892 Mr. Gladstone retired, and his place at the head of the Liberal Government was taken by Lord Rosebery. Lloyd George, in his efforts to secure the early passage of the Welsh disestablishment bill, continued to strike hard at his nominal chief until in 1894 came the end of this particular sphere of his operations, for the Liberal Government was turned out and a Conservative Government put in its place. This, however, was Lloyd George's real opportunity. Independent as he had been in the ranks of his own party, he now found far greater scope as a foe in opposition to Ministers in power. He went for them, tooth and nail, making a dead set at Chamberlain, who had taken Gladstone's place as the leading figure in the House of Commons. Chamberlain himself had fought his way up. Those who have seen Chamberlain will never forget him—the long, strong face, the steady, hard eyes, the straight-cut mouth, the rigidly erect, slim body, the unfailing single eyeglass, and the orchid in his buttonhole making a picture which can never be disassociated from will-power, a mind cold and clear, a lucid gift of speech, unflinching courage, and a savage contempt for weakness or inefficiency. He had against him in the House of Commons some able critics, but not more than two or three could really stand up to him in argument. I believe there was not a single one even of these who dared to take off the gloves to him in real fighting earnest. Lloyd George went into opposition with his eyes fixed on Chamberlain.

From that time onward Lloyd George deliberately fought the Birmingham statesman on every possible opportunity. In committee, during question time, at set debate, he pursued him unremittingly. Chamberlain tried at first to shake him off with a scornful word or two. But Lloyd George was not to be dismissed as so many others had been. He returned to the attack like a hornet. He was never appeased, never in doubt, never content. Chamberlain had presently to take real notice of him. He turned on the Welshman and with ferocity held him up to scorn and ridicule—not a difficult task for such a man as Chamberlain, especially as the majority of the House of Commons were his followers. Lloyd George certainly had his bad times then. Sometimes his facts would be proved awry and his arguments fallacious and he would be harried with merciless sarcasm. He would, in effect, be smashed to pieces. To the amazement of every one he refused to understand that he was smashed. After any and every attack he would be swiftly on his feet, hurling forth fresh accusatory words and ignoring the punishment he had just received—would be himself the scourger of sin. Sometimes he even took to imitating Chamberlain's own methods, and pointing a finger at his distinguished victim, would hiss out his charges word by word with a vibrant slowness. Even the impassive Chamberlain used sometimes to color a little under this mimicry. If ever a man went thoroughly out of his way to be hated it was Lloyd George. But he gained way. Once under an unsparing attack by Lloyd George, Chamberlain winced, leaped to his feet, and asked permission to make a second speech in reply. That was the first occasion which caused members to say among themselves that Chamberlain, gladiator that he was, had met his match in Lloyd George.

IV

THE DAREDEVIL STATESMAN

What was the underlying motive in Lloyd George during those years of feverish combat? Why should he have gone out of his way to deal injury and to incur enmity? Why was he always in the pose of rebel even when his friends were in power? Was he anything more than a clever young politician seeking notoriety by espousing unpopular courses whenever there was a chance to strike a blow at those high in authority? They are justifiable questions, and they can be answered quite shortly. Heaven had given Lloyd George, together with much impulsiveness, the most sensitive of souls and a kindly heart, together with the imagination of a poet. Even when he was a boy resentment blazed from him as he realized the injustices which were suffered by the poorer people, people who could not raise their voice to protest and who went on in stolid resignation from childhood to the grave. The example of his mother, a patient and noble woman, struggling with fate for the sake of her children, was ever before him. He saw his uncle, a sturdy Puritan of high character and intelligence, looked down upon, or at least disapproved of, because of his religious and political opinions, and this in spite of the fact that Richard Lloyd's beliefs sprang from selfless emotions and held him in an upright life. As Lloyd George grew older and mingled with the world he saw how oppression, active or passive, often went with wealth and power, and that not only material sustenance, but education and even the right to think, was denied the vast preponderance of the population by those who through inheritance, accident, or hardihood had secured the good things of the earth. Every nerve within him quivered in revolt. And even before he realized the full extent of the powers that lay within him his ardent spirit was leaping forward to fight what he regarded as the great giants of evil—the systems and the customs which gave individuals the power to hold down those who could not help themselves. He loved his native land passionately and was saturated with religious feeling, and he was strung with indignation that the state Church system of England should continue to be forced upon a nation of Nonconformists, with its resulting social influence on the people of his land. He was stirred to the depths by the lives of poor people among whom he had lived his most impressionable years. Enraged at the mental and moral attitude of the rich Conservatives who placidly assumed that Providence meant them to rule the earth and all the lesser horde to bow down to their inspired will, he was dissatisfied with the stolidity and lethargy of the official Liberal party, although he himself was a Liberal. When the Boer War broke out his sense of chivalry and justice was outraged at the thought that a great people like the British nation should attempt to crush a tiny pastoral race, even under some provocation. Thus from the start he devoted himself passionately and whole-heartedly to the side of the under dog.

Incidentally in this single-handed fight he took a sardonic delight in shocking those pillars of society who to him were symbols of the existing order of things. Fiercely he smashed away at idols, however highly placed, however much revered. At all times and in all circumstances he was regardless of consequences to himself, a fact which, together with his gifts, secured for him a certain measure of concealed respect even from those who hated him most. Withal, throughout these years of destructiveness his mind was working toward the formation of a new order of things. Behind and beyond all his Ishmaelitish tactics there were thoughts of a reconstruction. He may have been right or wrong in his courses. At any rate, it is necessary in a sketch of his career to set out the connecting links in years of activity which to a casual observer may seem disjointed, variable, and erratic.

A notable incident in his career was when, with practically the whole country inflamed against him, owing to his attitude on the Boer War, he decided to go down to Birmingham, the seat and stronghold of Joseph Chamberlain, and address a public meeting in support of his anti-war policy. Friends tried to dissuade him. He was not to be dissuaded. Preparations were quickly set afoot in Birmingham to break up his meeting. When the evening arrived so great were the hostile crowds around the town hall, so high their temper, that the chief constable of the city begged Lloyd George not to risk himself on the platform. Lloyd George would have none of his suggestion. He went to the hall, and his appearance was a signal for a riot such as had been unknown for a generation at a public gathering in Britain. In a frantic fight by the Chamberlain supporters to reach the platform the sympathizers with Lloyd George were trampled down. Furniture was broken up, windows were smashed, several people were seriously injured, and one man was killed. Lloyd George was smuggled out of the hall in a policeman's uniform.

England rang with the story of the happenings on that night in Birmingham. Lloyd George was called a coward and sneered at for allowing himself to get away in disguise, and if poisonous words could have checked a man's career he would have been finished from that time. A few days after the riot an M. P. met Joseph Chamberlain in the lobby of the House of Commons and said to him, "So your people didn't manage to kill Lloyd George the other night?" "What is everybody's business is nobody's business," said Chamberlain as he passed on.

It is a tribute to Lloyd George's power among his own people in Wales that when an election took place in the middle of the war he retained his seat in Parliament. You get a touch of the kind of man in the words he spoke to his supporters in the course of his speech after the declaration of the poll. "While England and Scotland are drunk with blood, the brain of Wales remains clear, and she advances with steady step on the road to progress and liberty."

The Conservatives remained in power to the end of 1905, and in the beginning of 1906 there was a general election which returned to power a strong Liberal majority augmented by some thirty Labor members. A vigorous spirit was sweeping through the Liberal ranks. New men had sprung to the front to take the place of those who had dropped out by death, old age, or the feeling that modern thought was too advanced for them. Sir Henry Campbell-Bannerman, a pawky old Scotsman who became the Liberal Prime Minister, did not confine the members of his Cabinet to the respectable leaders of old time, but brought in new blood, among his selections being Lloyd George. This promotion was unexpected by the public. Lloyd George had made a big reputation in Parliament, but it was always that of the free-lance. On vital questions of principle he was as free from control by the Liberals as by the Conservatives. He was known as an untamed guerrilla, and that was all. There were many shrugs of the shoulder, many doubtful whispers, at the hazards which Campbell-Bannerman was taking in putting such a person into the Cabinet. True, he was but one of the lesser appointments—namely, that of president of the Board of Trade—but was he capable of even that responsibility? Had he any capacity at all as an administrator? These were the doubts pretty freely expressed in political circles when the appointments to the new Cabinet were announced.

It is significant of the reserves in Lloyd George that from the time he took his place among the line of Ministers on the Treasury bench he began to show signs of qualities unsuspected. Gone was his combativeness. He answered questions about his department with urbanity, replied to criticism with courtesy and painstaking detail. Out of the House he devoted himself assiduously to learning the intricacies of his department. Very soon reforms began to be manifested. The Board of Trade, an old and historic department, largely bound up with red tape, became the most unconventional office in Whitehall. Moreover, the activities of the Board of Trade began to get an importance in Parliament that they had never hitherto possessed. Novel measures were brought in by Lloyd George and, what was more surprising, were successfully piloted into law by him. His grasp of detail, his unfailing tact, his readiness to meet reasonable objections, all contributed to the result. I do not mean that he was always suave, because occasionally biting sentences would make themselves felt as of old, but wherever courtesy and politeness were forthcoming from opponents he returned them in full measure. Responsibility was certainly having its effect on him.

He passed the Patents and Designs Act, formulated to compel manufacturers holding British patents to make their goods in Britain instead of abroad, and he passed also the Merchant Shipping Act, for the purpose of giving British sailors better food and healthier conditions of life. While the Board of Trade was thus forging its way in public estimation it suddenly became the most important Government department in the country. The railway men all over the lines planned a strike to get more pay, a strike which would have dislocated if it had not stopped all the trains in Britain. It is the business of the Board of Trade to handle labor disputes. Lloyd George was at once in the vortex. To the surprise of some, he took no extreme view, but considered it his duty as a Minister first of all to keep the railways running for the benefit of the community as a whole, and then after that to secure some arrangement, if it were possible, by which the lot of the railway men could be bettered. He flung into the struggle for compromise the whole of the ardor which for years past he had devoted to combat, and after ceaseless struggles with both sides during some days and nights he was successful in fixing up a scheme under which the railways were continued in operation, and the men got a good deal of what they asked for. All sections praised him, and the new Lloyd George was acclaimed as something of a revelation.

His tenure as president of the Board of Trade was his first experience as Cabinet Minister. He, nevertheless, established innovations the thought of which would have given respectable and long-established statesmen a shudder. He cared not a rap for convention. He was not in the least afraid of his permanent officials, who so often control their department and their political chief with it. A Cabinet Minister in Britain is hedged with a certain divinity and is almost unapproachable except under stated conditions. Lloyd George bewildered people with his approachability, his unpretentiousness. During the strain of the railway struggle he would exchange a cheery word with the waiting newspaper reporters as he passed them on going in or out of his office, an unheard-of thing for a Cabinet Minister to do. The second day was cold and inclement when he stopped among them as he approached the Board of Trade entrance. "There is no need for you gentlemen to wait outside here in the cold. Come inside and I'll find you a room," he said. He caused a comfortable apartment to be set aside for them during their vigil, and each afternoon he caused tea and cigarettes to be sent down to them to beguile the long period of waiting. Here is another little story of his early days of office. A railway smash at Shrewsbury resulted in the death of twenty people and the injury of a great many more, and in accordance with the usual practice the Board of Trade sent down immediately an inspector to investigate the cause of the accident. But on this occasion not only did the inspector go down to Shrewsbury, but his chief, the president of the Board of Trade, also, quite a novel course for a high and mighty Cabinet Minister. I was present as a journalist and remember seeing Lloyd George walking along by the side of the dismantled lines, threading his way through the wreckage, putting questions to the railway officials, and generally seeking to probe out on his own account how the affair occurred. On behalf of a score of special correspondents who had come down from London, I stopped Lloyd George in the street as he was walking to his hotel to ask him about the official inquiry. "Is it to be held in private, as usual?" I said. "No," replied Lloyd George. "The inquiry will be in public. Here are twenty people killed and the country has the right to know why they were killed." That was the way he used to break precedents. Next day we all went down to the Raven Hotel, the appointed place, and the inspector proceeded with his work of examining witnesses. Lloyd George sat by his side. I felt sorry for that inspector—who usually was monarch of all he surveyed. He was a man of dignified and leisurely manner. Lloyd George cut in and took the examination of witnesses out of his mouth and, figuratively speaking, turned them inside out in trying to get the facts. He did not consider the position of the inspector one bit. But he made the inquiry a very interesting one.

Despite his new manner on the Treasury bench in the House of Commons Lloyd George had lost none of the freshness and suppleness of mind which had distinguished him as a free-lance, and as he proceeded to do unexpected things it became apparent he was going to be as vital a figure in office as he had been on the back benches. Traces of appreciation showed themselves in public comment, though his ancient enemies, the Conservatives, held their dislike in reserve, and had some forebodings in their hearts about the future. They knew quite well by now that this Welshman could not be read at a glance.

Bits of the old Adam began to show up in Lloyd George's speeches as he lent his aid on the platform in support of Liberal proposals. I remember that at this time there was still a good deal of talk by the Conservatives of tariff reform—that is to say, of the imposition of import duties for protection and revenue purposes. The Liberals were against the proposals, fought them strongly, and indeed by their attitude had won a good deal of support in the election which returned them to power. Lloyd George made some of his flaming speeches in support of free trade against protection. Then came one night when the Board of Trade Minister had to speak in the House of Commons as a defender of the Government policy against a motion put forth by the Opposition in favor of tariff reform. After speakers on both sides had debated the topic for some hours it was Lloyd George's duty to wind up the discussion for the Government. When he rose there was much excitement on both sides and a good deal of shouting and counter-shouting. Remarks were thrown across from the Opposition benches indicating that Lloyd George's speeches about the evil of tariff reform on the Continent had been exaggerated. "I have been challenged," he said, "with regard to statements as to the food of the poorer people in Germany, and I am going to give now, not my opinion, but some hard facts." He held up a blue book. "This volume is the last annual report of the Consul-General in Germany. The facts which I shall quote are his facts, not mine. If you will not take my word, you will at any rate be able to take his word." He turned to a marked page. "Let us see what he says about a typical center, the city of Chemnitz. Here are some interesting figures as to what the poorer class eat in this tariff-reform paradise of Chemnitz." He proceeded to read extracts. I cannot recall the extra figures, but Lloyd George's phrases ran something like this: "This report states that in Chemnitz last year there were sold in the shops two thousand tons of horse-flesh. These are not my figures, mind, but those of the Consul-General. I commend the figures to excited members opposite. But horse-flesh is not the only thing the people through the pressure of tariff reform are compelled to eat in Chemnitz. They even eat dog-meat." (Cheers from the Liberals and derisive shouts from the Conservatives.) "The Consul-General states that one thousand tons of dog-meat were consumed in Chemnitz last year." (More shouting from both sides.) "But there is even worse to come." Lloyd George's voice took on a note of gravity, and the House hushed itself to listen. "Not only horse-flesh, not only dog-meat, but five hundred tons of donkey-flesh were sold in Chemnitz last year." He swung his finger along the line of Opposition leaders and paused. "The fact has a tragic significance for right honorable gentlemen who want to introduce tariff reform into this country."

Then his speech had to be suspended for a full minute.

At this time the cause of tariff reform was going rapidly downhill. Austen Chamberlain, the son of Joseph Chamberlain, strove hard to keep it to the fore, and frequently at intervals in the House of Commons the protectionist proposals were brought forward. Lloyd George had a characteristic word to say about the situation one day. "I do not blame Mr. Austen Chamberlain for sticking to his father. But the considerations which have made him protectionist are not fiscal, but filial. History ever repeats itself, and the boy still stands on the burning deck."

By rapid steps Lloyd George became the outstanding figure of the Government in which he occupied a comparatively minor position. Soon he was as prominent in Britain as, when a youth, he was prominent in Wales. Hardly a week passed in which he was not by his daring speeches or actions raising storms of anger among opponents or choruses of approval among the advanced Liberals. Vital force radiated from him. When Campbell-Bannerman died in 1908 and Asquith, his Chancellor of the Exchequer, became Prime Minister, it was on Lloyd George that his choice fell as the new Chancellor. The public, dazzled at Lloyd George's swift rise, withheld their judgment as to the wisdom of Mr. Asquith's experiment in this elevation of the Welshman to the post of second statesman in the United Kingdom. As for Lloyd George himself, he took up the position with calmness and a gleaming eye. At last he had his hand on the helm.

V

THE FIRST GREAT TASK

The biggest day in Lloyd George's life until he was called upon by the King to form a Government was Thursday, April 29, 1909. On that day he presented to Parliament and the country his first Budget—the framework of taxation and legislation which was to be the foundation of a new social system in Britain— which incidentally was to break the power of the House of Lords and to lead to such a storm among all classes that the aid of the King himself had to be invoked in order to carry out the plan of the Welsh statesman.

A dramatic situation had arisen at Westminster. Up to 1906 when the Liberals were returned by a large majority the Conservatives, with the exception of a short break, had been in power for twenty years. Another generation of the people had come to adult life since the early eighties when the Liberals were last in real power, and a new set of Liberal statesmen with advanced ideals had been put into office. The exultation among the forces of progress was great. The hot hopes were to have a speedy quenching. The laws of England are passed by the joint consent of the King, the House of Lords, and the House of Commons. The House of Commons is an electoral body, but the House of Lords has a hereditary membership, descending from father to son. Of the six hundred members of the House of Lords five hundred are Conservatives. The Conservative minority in the Commons, faced with startling Liberal reforms, called to their aid the five hundred stalwarts in the Lords, and the consequence was that the sweeping measures introduced by the Liberals were promptly thrown out by the Lords. Thus an intolerable situation presented itself to the Liberal majority chosen by the nation to direct its Government.

Lloyd George, on being appointed Chancellor of the Exchequer, at once set himself the task of meeting the difficulty, and there were weapons to his hand. He planned not only an elaborate scheme of reform, but also the means of putting it into execution in face of the House of Lords. The ostensible function of the Budget is to provide a schedule of taxation for the coming year in order to meet the current needs of the country. Lloyd George's plan was to put forward his own conception of "the needs of the country" and then to raise the money on account of them. He purposed to bring about a wholesale readjustment between rich and poor and to use the readjustment as a basis for developments in the future. That was his bold and carefully devised plan of action. It will be asked at once why the Lords could not frustrate this intention as well as those embodied in the other Liberal bills they had thrown out. This was the reason: the Lords were prevented by the constitution from altering money bills sent up to them by the Commons, though they might do what they liked with other bills. The people provided the taxes, the Commons are elected by the people, and the power of the purse possessed by the Commons gives the people the command in affairs of state. As long ago as the time of Charles II. this rule about the Commons and Lords with respect to money supplies was emphatically laid down. Lloyd George's scheme was to wrap up social changes in his Budget and to dare the Lords to meddle with them, inasmuch as they were part and parcel of a money bill.

The country had no idea of this deep-rooted plan. Something sensational was expected of Lloyd George, but his proposals, it was thought, would be of a purely financial nature, including, possibly, heavy taxation of rich people and relief of the indirect taxation of the poor. As a matter of fact, Lloyd George, walking over from Downing Street to the House of Commons on that Thursday afternoon, had three secrets in the leather despatch-case he carried in his hand. One was the amount of money he was going to raise, the second the sources from which he was going to obtain it, and third the way in which the money was to be spent. Those of us who saw him walking briskly across Palace Yard that afternoon in company with Mr. Winston Churchill little thought that the small brown despatch-case held plans which within three years were to alter vitally the constitution of the United Kingdom as it had existed for eight hundred years.

The national financial position was known in the morning before Lloyd George made his speech. The amount needed for the current year by the country for the army, navy, civil services, and social relief was 164,152,000 pounds. The revenue to be expected on the existing basis of taxation was 148,390,000 pounds. A deficit of nearly 16,000,000 pounds had, therefore, to be provided for. In addition, in the framing of this as of other Budgets, regard was necessary to the automatic increase of certain expenditures in coming years, increases which must be met by the expanding capacity of schemes of revenue. (Though the Budget is an annual affair, a good many of its features are necessarily continuing.) After all this has been taken into account there must be remembered that Lloyd George was planning still further expenditure. He had therefore to get piles of money from somewhere or other and to make sure of it in increasing volume as years went on.

I was present in the House of Commons to describe the Budget scene. The Chamber was packed and was quivering with excitement when at four minutes to three, during the preliminary business, Lloyd George, with a red despatch-box in his hand, came into view from behind the Speaker's chair, and passed with alert and nervous steps to the place on the Treasury bench reserved for him between the Prime Minister, Mr. Asquith, and Mr. Churchill. I can see Lloyd George now as he sat bolt-upright with one knee crossed over the other, waiting for the moment when the chairman should call on him. His face was pale and his eyes were rather dull. He looked a little overwrought. He was feeling the tension; so much was obvious. I remember wondering if he had reached the limit of his strength, whether he was really big enough in spirit for the ordeal that lay before him.

Within ten minutes the formal business of the day was over, and the chairman, standing up on his dais, announced, "Mr. Chancellor of the Exchequer." Lloyd George rose to the table. He seemed almost an insignificant figure in the midst of the crowded assembly. Members were filling all the seats, some squatting on the steps of the Speaker's chair, others standing together in the space below the bar at the farther end of the House. The galleries banked overhead were occupied by distinguished visitors, foreign ambassadors, members of the House of Lords, ladies of title, distinguished men of thought and action. It was such an audience as is given to but few men in a lifetime.

In low voice and conversational phrase Lloyd George began his speech. He told of the money that had to be raised, but he did not stop at the narrative of what may be called ordinary expenditure. He told how the primary duty of a rich nation was to help those who had been exhausted, to give a chance to the downtrodden. He related some of the things he had in his mind—the insurance of workmen against illness and unemployment, the payment of pensions for persons over a certain age. He told of how unemployment might be largely eliminated by developments in the countryside, through new methods of agriculture, through light railways, through afforestation, through stock-breeding, through the reclamation of land. Efforts in these directions would not only help a great many of the population at the present time, but would provide enormously increased opportunities for coming generations. He proposed that part of the money of the year should be taken up with these projects.

Very soon he swept into the explanation of how new money was to be raised. It was necessary to set up a system which would, year by year, produce an increasing supply of money. When Lloyd George came to the point of his actual proposals you could have heard the slightest rustle of an order paper, so keen were the silent Commons. He was going to raise the income tax, he said, the existing impost on incomes of 160 pounds a year and over. He was going to put a super tax on rich people, those who had 5,000 pounds a year or more. He was going to make big additions to the duty charged on great estates when they changed hands.

Demand after demand he showered on the rich and comfortable. The assembly, expecting surprises, had them in abundance. The Chancellor drew sheaf after sheaf of notes from the red despatch-box on the table in front of him and explained with an air of intensive reasonableness the huge sums he proposed to draw from the property-owners in the country. New inroads were to be made on the profits of land and liquor. Coal-mines were to pay royalties. People were to be taxed when they became rich without any effort on their own part, but by fortunate accident in the increased value of special localities. There was to be a complete valuation of every yard of land in the country as the basis for developments to come.

Although the money to be raised that year by these new proposals would not much more than cover what was required by immediate necessities, the taxation was such as to multiply in product as years went on. Finally the motive behind the revolutionary Budget of Lloyd George came in the concluding words of his speech. "It is essential that we should make provision for the defense of our country. But, surely, it is equally imperative that we should make it a country even better worth defending for all and by all. And it is that this expenditure is for both these purposes that alone can justify the Government. I am told that no Chancellor of the Exchequer has ever been called upon to impose such heavy taxes in a time of peace. This, Mr. Chairman, is a war Budget. It is for raising money to wage implacable warfare against poverty and squalidness. I cannot help hoping and believing that before this generation has passed away we shall have advanced a great step toward that good time when poverty and wretchedness, and the human degradation which always follows in its camp, will be as remote from the people of this country as the wolves which once infested its forests."

It took a day or so for the full effect of the Budget to be understood. And then enthusiasm rose in the breasts of Liberals and Labor men, while the middle and upper classes poured forth outcries and protests. As the proposals were discussed in detail, feeling arose on both sides, and Lloyd George was variously described as a genius who was laying the foundation of a new Britain and a predatory politician out to catch votes. Throughout the length and breadth of the United Kingdom his name was on the lips of all, either in execration or in praise.

The greatest Parliamentary fight of a generation began to take form in the House of Commons. The Conservatives, led by Mr. Balfour, put up an obstructive fight to every line and almost every word of the finance bill which was founded on the Budget. Departmental duties all day, the onward fight with his finance measure throughout the night and often the early hours of the morning, became the routine of Lloyd George's life. I have seen him at the table at the House of Commons at seven o'clock in the morning, with ashen face and burning eyes, after a week of all-night sittings, persuading, explaining, and arguing with determined opponents of his measure. Often enough in these fatiguing morning hours there would be sitting up behind the grille in the ladies' gallery an anxious, but proud, woman watching the Welsh statesman at the table. It was Mrs. George, the pretty Maggie Owen of years before whom the young Welsh solicitor had taken from her father's farm.

In justice I ought to summarize in a few sentences written at the time the attitude of the opponents of the Budget. "Why put forward these extraordinary changes? Here was an unequaled nation, the richest and greatest in existence, which by its character and energy had built up an empire reaching across the globe, with Parliamentary institutions which were the admiration of every state. The millions of our population were welded in a common sentiment, unsurpassed since history began, making unshakable the foundations of our nationality. We had fought our way to modern conditions very slowly, and now, class for class, we were perhaps the most contented and prosperous people on the face of the earth. Admitted that we had vast crowds of silently enduring poor. (The poor we have always with us, as has every great nation.) But the way to ameliorate the evils among them was not to disturb the comfort, convenience, or property of the rich, but to increase the prosperity of rich and poor alike by putting a tax on foreigners' goods coming into this country, thus providing revenue and increasing home manufactures at one stroke. That was the course to pursue, not to disturb the elaborate and happy system, the pride of the world, by sudden incursions into the liberty of the individual and by depredations on the privileged in order to benefit the unhappy. Property, whether obtained without effort or built up by the hardest of labor, had its inalienable rights, and violently to outrage those rights was not only unjust to the persons chiefly concerned, but dangerous to the state at large."

The campaign which was set in motion against Lloyd George has not been equaled in violence since the old free-speaking days of a century ago. He was called a vulgar Welsh attorney. He was accused of having every kind of attribute which was contemptible and hateful. One of the things urged against him was that he was no gentleman and could not understand the feeling of gentlefolk, owing to his unfortunate upbringing. His opponents thus attacking him went into paroxysms of rage over a speech he made at Limehouse in the East End of London, where he defended his Budget. The Limehouse speech has become famous as an example of Lloyd George's oratory. I give a few extracts to enable an idea to be formed about it.

"The Budget is introduced, not merely for the purpose of raising barren taxes, but taxes that are fertile taxes, taxes that will bring forth fruit—the security of the country which is paramount in the minds of all, provision for the aged and deserving poor. It was time it was done. It is rather a shame for a rich country like ours, probably the richest country in the world, if not the richest the world has ever seen, that it should allow those who have toiled all their days to end in penury and possibly starvation. It is rather hard that an old workman should have to find his way to the gates of the tomb, bleeding and footsore through the brambles and thorns of poverty. We cut a new path through, an easier one, a pleasanter one, through fields of waving corn. We are raising money to pay for the new road, aye, and to widen it, so that two hundred thousand paupers shall be able to join in the march. There are many in the country blessed by Providence with great wealth, and if there are among them men who grudge out of their riches a fair contribution toward the less fortunate of their fellow-countrymen, they are shabby rich men.

"We propose to do more by the means of the Budget. We are raising money to provide against the evils and sufferings that follow from unemployment. We are raising money for the purpose of assisting our great friendly societies to provide for the sick, the widows, and the orphans. We are providing money to enable us to develop the resources of our own land. I do not believe any fair-minded man would challenge the justice and the fairness of the objects which we have in view of raising this money. But there are some who say that the taxes themselves are unjust, unfair, unequal, oppressive, notably so the land taxes. They are engaged, not merely in the House of Commons, but outside the House of Commons, in assailing these taxes with a concentrated and sustained ferocity which will not even allow a comma to escape with its life.

"We claim that the tax we impose on land is fair, just, and moderate. They go on threatening that if we proceed they will cut down their benefactions and discharge labor. What kind of labor? What is the labor they are going to choose for dismissal? Are they going to threaten to devastate rural England while feeding themselves and dressing themselves? Are they going to reduce their gamekeepers? That would be sad. The agricultural laborer and the farmer might then have some part of the game which they fatten with their labor. But what would happen to you in the season? No weekend shooting with the Duke of Norfolk for any of us. But that is not the kind of labor they are going to cut down. They are going to cut down productive labor—builders and gardeners—and they are going to ruin their property so that it shall not be taxed. All I can say is this: the ownership of land is not merely an enjoyment, it is stewardship. It has been reckoned as such in the past, and if they cease to discharge their functions, which include the security and defense of the country and the looking after the broken in their villages and neighborhood, those functions which are part of the traditional duties attaching to the ownership of land and which have given to it its title, if they cease to discharge those functions, the time will come to reconsider the conditions under which land is held in this country. No country, however rich, can permanently afford to have quartered upon its revenue a class which declines to do the duty which it is called upon to perform. And, therefore, it is one of the prime duties of statesmanship to investigate those conditions.

"We are placing the burdens on the broad shoulders. Why should I put burdens on the people? I am one of the children of the people. I was brought up among them. I know their trials, and God forbid that I should add one grain of trouble to the anxiety which they bear with such patience and fortitude. When the Prime Minister did me the honor of inviting me to take charge of the national Exchequer at a time of great difficulty I made up my mind in framing the Budget which was in front of me that at any rate no cupboard should be barer, no lot should be harder to bear. By that test I challenge them to judge the Budget."

The passion among the middle classes and the upper classes rose to such a pitch against Lloyd George's proposals as to cause more than one serious and religiously minded person to write and express wonder that Heaven did not strike dead such a wicked man before he could accomplish his fell purpose in the ruin of the country.

There is a story told about a man who jumped from the pier at Brighton into the sea to rescue a drowning person. In describing his experience the rescuer said: "It was easy enough. Only a few strokes were necessary to reach him. I got hold of him by the collar just as he was going down. Having turned him over on his back to see that it wasn't Lloyd George, I then brought him to the pier."

The House of Lords felt they had the country behind them, and they proceeded to the unprecedented and unconstitutional course of killing the Budget. This was exactly what Mr. Asquith and his first lieutenant had been waiting for. Lloyd George saw the fruits of his labor destroyed in a day, but he watched the process, not with despair, but with grim satisfaction.

The Lords had broken their last Liberal bill, for Lloyd George had determined to break the Lords.

VI

HOW LLOYD GEORGE BROKE THE HOUSE OF LORDS

A few days later, with Lloyd George sitting by his side, Mr. Asquith, the Prime Minister, made the following announcement in Parliament: "The House of Commons would, in the judgment of his Majesty's Government, be unworthy of its past and of the traditions of which it is the custodian and trustee if it allowed another day to pass without making it clear that it does not mean to brook the greatest indignity and the most arrogant usurpation to which for more than two centuries it has been asked to submit. We have advised the Crown to dissolve Parliament at the earliest possible moment."

The preparations for the general election included a campaign of vilification against Lloyd George which shook even some of the Conservatives. But the Chancellor of the Exchequer, on the other hand, was not disturbed, and he did not hesitate to do a little vilification on his own account. "What a low creature!" was the instant retort to any incursions of this kind.

One of the secrets of Lloyd George's career was that he always made his opponents too angry to appraise him correctly. They simply couldn't do it. A little cold-blooded study of him and his past history would have served them well. Because Lloyd George had a peculiarly bitter tongue and a peculiarly stimulating one he was abused as a fluent demagogue with nothing but unscrupulous and violent words to give him prominence. This was not a mere pretense on the part of the upper classes. They seriously believed it. As a result Lloyd George had a tremendous pull over the whole lot of them. One secret of his power was that his real strength lay not in words, but in his capacity for action. Because he talked about things with recklessness and force it was assumed that he could not do things. The hard fact was that he was more effective in doing things and in getting them done than in talking about them. He secured a wonderful advantage from all this. While hard names were being showered on him, and even while he was replying to them, he was at work quietly. I have often thought that as soon as his opponents found him out they felt that this was not fair, that he ought to have played the game and to have shown himself as exactly the kind of man they had portrayed him to be. Yet, at the time, his enemies would probably have been contemptuous of the suggestion that this ranting person could possibly be a man who was specially gifted in carrying plots and plans and big state projects into execution. They had to learn to their cost that he was both resolute and stealthy.

Lloyd George had as his chief Mr. Asquith, a man of crystal intellect, who had won high distinction, first at his university, than at the bar, where he was a famous advocate, and latterly in the House of Commons, where his mastery of Parliamentary arts was only equaled by that of the rival leader, Mr. Balfour. His speeches were powerful, but they appealed to the head rather than to the emotions. Unlike Lloyd George, he was not by way of being a prophet. He could not by sheer intensity sway the House of Commons. Mr. Asquith, moreover, was quite incapable of stirring a public audience on the platform outside the House, and he lacked that terrific energy which distinguished his principal colleague. But he was, nevertheless, a first-rate partner. His steady, cold brain would carry into effect with precision an intricate, delicate, and bold plan of operations. He had hardihood. Every wile in public life was known to him. He had strong will-power. And in sheer brain of what may be called the purely intellectual type he was miles ahead, not only of Lloyd George, but of all the other politicians of the day. I should say here that he undoubtedly felt deeply the slur cast upon the House of Commons by the Lords. And there is one more trait that should be mentioned, his unshakable loyalty to those who served under him, and to his brilliant Chancellor of the Exchequer not less than to any of the others.

It implies, however, no disrespect to Mr. Asquith to say that he had become the instrument of Lloyd George. It was the latter's subtle brain that evolved the possible consequences which might ensue after his first stroke in the Budget of April, 1909. It was his bold spirit that urged the desperate course which was presently pursued. He measured the Lords and decided that if they could not be frightened into defeat they could be hustled into a wild attempt which would be equally disastrous to them.

Joyfully he entered the fray as soon as the Lords threw out the Budget. In a public speech made immediately after the Lords' action he said: "I come here to-day not to preach a funeral oration. I am here neither to bury nor to praise the Budget. If it is buried it is in the sure and certain hope of a glorious resurrection. As to its merits, no one appreciates them more sincerely than I do, but its slaughter has raised greater, graver, and more fruitful issues. We have got to arrest the criminal. We have to see he perpetrates no further crime. A new chapter is now being written for the sinister assembly which is more responsible than any other power for wrecking popular hopes, but which, in my judgment, has perpetrated its last act of destructive fury. They have slain the Budget. In doing so they have killed the bill which, if you will permit me to say so, had in it more promises of better things for the people of this country than most things which have been submitted to the House of Commons. It made provision against the inevitable evils which befall such large masses of our poor population, through old age, infirmity, sickness, and unemployment. The schemes of which the Budget was the small foundation would, in my judgment, if they had been allowed to fructify, have eliminated at least hunger from the terrors that haunt the workman's cottage. Yet here you have an order of men blessed with every fortune which Providence can bestow on them grudging a small pittance out of their super-abundance in order to protect those who have built up their wealth against the haunting terror of misery and despair. They have thrown it out, and in doing so they have initiated one of the greatest, gravest, and most promising struggles of the time. Liberty owes as much to the foolhardiness of its foes as it does to the sapience and wisdom of its friends. At last the case between the peers and the people has been set down for trial in the great assize of the people, and the verdict will be given soon."

The country was quickly in the midst of the election. It cannot be said that Lloyd George dealt lightly with the House of Lords. Here is a typical reference: "Who are the guardians of this mighty British people? I shall have to make exceptions, but they are men who have neither the training, the qualifications, nor the experience which would fit them for such a gigantic task. The majority of them are simply men whose sole qualification is that they are the first-born of persons who had just as little qualifications as themselves. To invite this imperial race, this, the greatest commercial nation in the world, the nation that has taught the world in the principles of self-government and liberty—to invite this nation itself to sign a decree that declares itself unfit to govern itself without the guardianship of such people, that is an insult which I hope will be thrown back with ignominy."

Not only the upper classes, but a great many of the lower classes stormed and raged at these and similar words. The *Daily Mail* went so far as to give a column of titbits from Lloyd George's speeches in order to show what a really vulgar and detestable person he was, and how unfit to occupy any leading position in the state.

The election results as they began to come in indicated that while the Liberals were losing a number of seats which in years gone by had been Conservative strongholds, they were, nevertheless, going to retain the confidence of the country. In the result Mr. Asquith found himself once again in command of the House of Commons with a majority of one hundred and twenty-four.

The cards were placed in the hands of the Liberals now, but they had to be very carefully played. The House of Lords swallowed its humiliation as best it could and passed the famous Budget on April 28, 1910, exactly one year after its introduction into the House of Commons. They did not make any fuss about it, because, as I shall show, they had other things to think of. I remember the day on which the bill became law in the House of Lords. There were very few peers present. Several of the members of the House of Commons walked across from the Commons to witness the culmination of their effort. Among them was Lloyd George. He came in under the gallery, sprucely dressed in a morning coat, his long hair brushed back from his forehead and above his ears with a neatness which was not observable in his moments of excitement. To-day he had no work to do: one job was finished and he was only on the threshold of another. As he stood at the bar he looked over the members of the House of Lords with a grave and benignant expression which reminded one of a fond father regarding erring children. I thought of the studious expression which usually characterized the face of that daredevil boy down at Llanystumdwy all those years ago. I am quite sure that the peers who observed him surveying them did not think he was benignant. If I am any judge of feelings, they looked upon him, as he stood there at the bar, as a particularly malignant type of viper. With a genial smile Lloyd George exchanged a chatty word or two with an M. P. at his side. No one would have guessed that there was bitterness in his soul at this assembly or that with grim purpose he was even now marking out the destruction of their powers.

It is the fashion in the House of Lords to give the King's consent to legislation by proxy. The consent, moreover, is given now, as for many hundreds of years past, not in the English language, but in the language of the old Norman-French conqueror of nearly a thousand years ago. A bewigged clerk read out in resonant tones the title of the bill and from another official there came the answer of the King, "Le Roy le veult" ("The King wills it"). The Budget of 1909 had become part of the law of the United Kingdom. Lloyd George, still chatting cheerfully with a fellow-member of the House of Commons, walked back to the Lower Chamber.

If any of the Lords thought that the threats used against them in the course of the election meant nothing and were only a kind of bluster to get the Budget passed, they were grievously mistaken. It must have been hard for them to realize that Lloyd George meant all the presumptuous things he said. He was never more in earnest. A cut-and-dried plan had been arranged between him and Mr. Asquith with regard to the Lords. The plan was no less than this—to take away from the peers their constitutional rights to do more than to hold up for three successive sessions any legislation passed by the House of Commons. They were not to have the power of killing bills, though they might retard them a little. And so far as money bills were concerned they were not to be allowed to delay them at all. The Commons were to be given power to pass any money bill over the head of the Lords if the latter did not agree to it immediately it was sent up to them. In these cases the King and Commons between them were to be the lawmaking power, and as the King's assent is always automatically given to the proposals of Ministers in power the net result would be the complete supremacy of the Commons in Government.

But how were these changes to be made effective? They could, of course, only be brought into force by legal enactment, and it was impossible to expect the Lords to sign their own death warrant. It was settled between Lloyd George and Mr. Asquith to take the House of Lords by the throat. Lloyd George was prepared for extreme measures, and Mr. Asquith, a student of English history, found out a way by means of ancient precedent. Twice before in the story of the British Parliament there had been similar episodes. In the reign of Queen Anne and in the reign of William IV. the Prime Minister of the day, encountering opposition from the House of Lords, had gone to the reigning sovereign and secured the promise of the creation of enough new peers to turn the minority in the House of Lords into a preponderance of votes. This was the plan now agreed upon, only the audacity of it was far greater than on previous occasions, because Queen Anne's new peers numbered but twelve and the number of new peers proposed to be created in 1832 to pass the Reform bill under William IV. was limited to eighty. Mr. Asquith and Lloyd George faced the fact that on this occasion it would be necessary to create something like five hundred new peers.

I pass over some of the intervening stages—the howls that came from the Lords, who saw their prestige departing with this wholesale dilution of their order; the choking attempts which the peer leaders made to be civil of tongue and to arrange a compromise. Merciless was the determination of Lloyd George.

Another general election on the specific issue of the power of the Lords again resulted in the return of the Liberals to office.

The Government proposals for the restriction of the future functions of the Lords were embodied in a measure called the Parliament bill, and it was for the Lords to pass this measure or else to suffer the immediate creation of the army of new peers who had been nominated by Mr. Asquith and who would immediately vote down the existing Conservative majority in the gilded chamber.

The climax was reached on August 9, 1911, when the bill, having passed through the Commons, was brought up to the House of Lords for their decision. The peers by this time were torn between two impulses. One, the most natural, was to defy Mr. Asquith and Lloyd George and all their wicked companions, and let them create what peers they liked, and the other to swallow the medicine, pass the Parliament bill, and thus, while limiting their own powers for the future, preserve their ancient caste and dignity.

It was touch and go throughout an excited discussion. Lord Morley, plain John Morley of the years gone by, made a speech of three sentences in which he said he was authorized to state that the King would assent to the creation of the extra peers if the bill were not passed. Wild hopes that the King would stand by the Lords were thus extinguished. There were dramatic scenes never to be forgotten by those who witnessed them, and then finally the bill was accepted by a majority of seventeen votes. The power of the House of Lords, strong for centuries, had been broken. The man who had broken it was Lloyd George.

VII

AT HOME AND IN DOWNING STREET

In the midst of all the stormy times of the fight with the House of Lords and afterward up to the present moment Lloyd George's personal life in its simplicity and happiness has been a standing contrast to the turmoil and passion of his public energy. Meet Lloyd George among his family, and it is hard to realize that such a homely, genial person could be the man who tackled so rancorously the House of Lords. I went to 11 Downing Street one day after the Budget fight was over, and when, as Chancellor of the Exchequer, Lloyd George was preparing further legislative changes. Eleven Downing Street, it should be explained, is the official residence of the Chancellor of the Exchequer and joins number 10, where the Prime Minister lives. It is a dingy, ugly-looking building, attractive only by reason of its associations. In the year that America declared her independence number 10 Downing Street was the residence of Lord North, and it may then, as now, have had connecting doors which made the two houses into practically one official home.

Lloyd George discussed public affairs in a corner of the old library lined with books which Gladstone used to consult half a century ago and his predecessors before him. A glance round the rows of volumes, nearly all of them ponderous and many of them venerable, caused me to ask Lloyd George who was his favorite author. He gave me no philosopher, not even a poet, in reply. "I like romance," he said, "historical romance. I am fond of Dumas and of modern writers like Stanley Weyman." Possibly Lloyd George has never looked into those old, handsome, leather-covered volumes at his official residence. His secretaries may have pondered over them in securing material for their chief, but Lloyd George has been too busy doing things to devote much time to ancient philosophical reflections or to learned economic theories. It is easy to understand how his temperament found satisfaction and relaxation at the same time in the cut-and-thrust work of Dumas and Weyman. I ought, perhaps, to add that he explained with a smile how politics did not leave him much time for serious reading just then. They have certainly left him still less since that time.

We were in the thick of talk about the busy political era when a little girl of twelve, with a ribbon of blue round her tumbling hair, came running into the room, not knowing that a visitor was present. She would have run out again, upon seeing me, if her father had not stopped her and caught her into his arms. For the rest of the interview she sat on his knee, listening with big, live eyes to the conversation. Once she cuddled closer to her father and laughed merrily as he confessed to me that his next bill before Parliament was one to prohibit the holidays of little girls at school from lasting more than six weeks. Megan was the darling of her father's heart. Two or three mornings of the week you could have seen them hand in hand walking from 11 Downing Street across St. James's Park to watch the ducks feeding in the lake. With sparkling blue eyes, a sensitive mouth, and vivacious manner, little Megan had some of her father's characteristics. She was a daughter any father might be proud of. I guarantee Lloyd George was prouder of her—and still is—than of his epoch-making Budget or his historic victory over the House of Lords. Just now in Parliamentary session, or indeed out of it, Lloyd George has not very much time for walks in the parks—but I am sure Megan gets her share of attention in spite of the European war.

The war has, of course, intensified Lloyd George's life and somewhat altered its channels, but its main directions are preserved. At all hours of day and night he must be prepared for service. He could not, however, carry on his work without proper rest and sleep, and the following is the kind of routine to which he has accustomed himself. Awakening at seven in the morning, he has a quick glance through the principal newspapers, not only of London, but those from the provinces and from abroad as well. Occasionally while he is dressing, and always before he leaves his room, he looks through documents and papers which he has brought up to his bedside on the previous night. (They are arranged in their proper order on a table by the side of his bed so that in any waking fit at night he can put his hand on them readily.)

Visitors begin to arrive early, because Lloyd George has re-established the practice of Victorian statesmen in having guests to breakfast with him and his family. By this means he not only saves time from many social functions, but gets through a lot of business as well, for his breakfast guests include politicians, editors, leading officials, prominent travelers from overseas, indeed practically the whole range of persons who for state or private reasons he desires to meet.

Soon after ten o'clock he is busy with his secretaries. These have already been at work on the morning letters, which in the days when he was Chancellor of the Exchequer numbered a thousand a day and are now probably three or four times as many. Work of a widely different kind keeps Lloyd George on the go till lunch-time—departmental conferences, visits from or to Cabinet Ministers, the supervision of answers to questions to be put to him in the House of Commons that afternoon, the reception of deputations from various interests affected by current proposals or future proposals that he is making. At least once a week, and sometimes more frequently, there is a Cabinet meeting in the morning that probably lasts well into the afternoon. On days when there is no Cabinet meeting there will be other visitors at lunch-time, and these are generally of an official character. Big plans affecting the social future of England have undoubtedly been worked out over Lloyd George's lunch-table. He is a vivid talker himself, but he is also a good listener, and there is not any one more ready to give an ear to tactful and helpful advice—only those who offer it must have something to say.

At a quarter to three in the afternoon the House of Commons assembles, and from that time onward to eleven o'clock at night Lloyd George is to be found either on the Treasury bench or in his private room behind the Speaker's chair. Endless are the occupations for a busy Minister in Parliament, and whether he is answering questions, expounding policy, fighting through details of proposals, or merely listening to the speeches of opponents, he is pretty well on the stretch the whole time. Even in his own room there is business to be done, deputations to be received, "whips" to be consulted, friendly or hostile talks to be gone through with members, and frequently also the reception of individual visitors. All this takes no account of social usages, the little hospitalities which must not be forgotten—the accompanying of groups of constituents to the public galleries, the entertainment of other groups to tea on the Terrace overlooking the river. Sometimes an hour may be seized for the House of Lords at the other end of the corridor when they are dealing with Commons legislation.

I asked Lloyd George how he managed to sleep after such days as these, and he said: "I never have any difficulty about that. Downing Street is only about four minutes' walk from the House of Commons. If the House adjourns at eleven I am usually away by twenty minutes past, and at a quarter to twelve I am in bed—probably asleep. This power for quick sleep has always been a great help to me."

The Lloyd George family at home consisted of Mr. and Mrs. George, two sons, and two daughters. Of the two boys, both in the twenties, one was at Cambridge University and the other in a responsible position as a civil engineer. Both are now soldiers, fighting in France. There are two girls, Megan and her sister, Olwen, a charming girl who has lately become engaged to a medical officer in the army. There is another person who frequently completes the family circle at 11 Downing Street. It is Richard Lloyd, the old shoemaker who forty years ago risked his little all to educate his orphan nephew. It was one of the pleasurable anticipations of Lloyd George, when he was appointed Chancellor of the Exchequer with the privileges of this historic residence, that Richard Lloyd would be able to come and stay there. "My dear old uncle," he said, "will be so proud to come and stay at the house in which Gladstone, his great hero, at one time lived."

Lloyd George is wiry, but no man, however strong, could continue indefinitely to put himself under such a strain as I have indicated without occasional complete rest. When he is not under too heavy a time he will go for a weekend's golf to Walton Heath, some twenty miles from London, in Surrey, or spend a couple of days at Brighton on the south coast. But when he is really exhausted there is only one place for him, and that is his beautiful home near Criccieth, about a mile from Llanystumdwy, where he spent his boyhood. On the hills rising from behind Criccieth and forming the foot of the Snowdon range he has built a graceful residence, whence he can look down over the wooded slopes to Criccieth and thence to Carnarvon Bay. On the other side the house faces the snow-capped mountains. From every window there is a beautiful scene. A lane leading from the gates, between towering hedges, winds through fields and woods down to Llanystumdwy.

With the charm of mountains, countryside, and sea there goes an invigorating atmosphere. "When I am exhausted," said Lloyd George to me once, "I come down here from London and I sleep long nights. In the daytime I sit out here on the veranda in a basket-chair with a rug around me, facing the sea, and here I rest and sometimes sleep. This beautiful Welsh air wraps me all round with its healing touch, and I let it do its work, and I am soon well again." During these recuperative days Lloyd George does no business, writes no letters, receives no visitors, sees no one but members of his own family. After about three days of this treatment he is recovering himself.

One day in a lane near Criccieth I met him in tweed suit and soft gray hat, with field-glasses strapped around him, and a stout walking-stick in his hand. He had been at Criccieth a fortnight, and thoughts of work were again seizing hold of him. He had in prospect a big scheme of land legislation that was to continue and develop the movement begun in the Budget. (A little later the war cut the project short.) "I am going for a walk up to the mountains," he said. "I can do my thinking best when I am out walking alone." Afterward I wondered what new revolution to startle the landed aristocracy of Britain he devised on that summer day by himself among the mountains. Curiously enough, Lloyd George does not like exercise for his own sake, but he enjoys it when he has a mental task in hand; he also enjoys it during a game of golf. I once heard him say that without golf he would never have thought of taking a four-mile walk for recreation. It is worthy of mention in connection with this that he has been described at second hand on his own confession as being a very lazy man, and that he has sometimes absolutely to force himself to a settled task—and, strange as it may appear, there is nothing in this inconsistent with the public estimation of him as a person of uncontrollable energy. Let his heart be given to an object, and there is no effort he will spare, no degree of fatigue to which he will not drive himself.

Intensely fond of an open-air life, Lloyd George's days at Criccieth are always a joy to him. You will come across him unexpectedly on the bank of the river Dwyfor with a fishing-rod in his hand, trying for trout. You will see him sometimes in the early morning at work in his garden in his endeavor to demonstrate that fruit trees will grow as well in Welsh soil as in the warm, red earth of Devonshire. Sometimes he and his wife, with perhaps one of his sons, will put a couple of tents into an automobile, start off up among the mountains, and camp out in some lonely and romantic spot for days at a time, living the primitive life entirely by themselves.

Strange it is to observe the attitude of the people of the countryside where he was brought up and where he built his early fame. There are a scattered few of the middle classes who in this remote country spot cannot understand the heights he has reached in public estimation. It is really a weird sensation to come from the outer world and talk to these people. No, no, he may to some extent have secured notoriety in circles even as far off as London, but really there is nothing in the man. Why, he was brought up here in the village! But these quaintly prejudiced folk are, after all, but a remnant, and the great mass of people all around in the farms and cottages prize his fame highly. The pride with which a villager refers to the fact that he went to school with Mr. Lloyd George must be one of the highest pleasures experienced by the Welsh statesman. It is an event to go to a meeting in the institute at Llanystumdwy and hear him address a crowded meeting of his compatriots in their native tongue and with all the old affectionate familiarity of a long-standing friend and neighbor. The rolling music of the ancient language is echoed back from the enthusiastic Celts in a kind of rhythmic ecstasy which thrills even the ignorant and alien Sassenach visitor. Lloyd George is still one of themselves. It is indeed hard for them to realize his position in the outside world, though they are so proud of it. To Criccieth and Llanystumdwy he is not so much the prominent statesman of the United Kingdom as just Lloyd George, the friend who grew up with them. He will never be anything else to them. It is all quite delightful and, one may add, quite bewildering to his enemies, who cannot understand that such unconcealed and regardless simplicity is an integral part of the nature of him whom they regard as a malignant. I have seen Lloyd George in a hundred capacities, electrifying a multitude, in the thick of battle with the cleverest minds of Parliament, attacking to their faces with relentless ferocity men of the noblest descent in Britain, and yet I know of nothing in his life which approaches in interest his relations with his old village friends of long ago. They like him for himself and not for what he has become, though they are so proud of him. One elderly lady, a friend of the Lloyd George family, when paying a visit to London heard that Lloyd George was to address a London meeting, and she thought she would like to go and hear him. She presented herself at the hall and was nearly swept off her feet by the surging crowd making its way in. After reaching one of the corridors with difficulty, she got an attendant to take her name in to Mrs. Lloyd George. The latter, who was on the platform, hurried out to her old friend and took her to a seat in the front of the hall. The building was packed in every part. Lloyd George got one of his usual receptions and made one of his usual speeches. The old lady was staggered. She went back to Wales full of the wonderful experience—and it has to be remembered that she had known Lloyd George all her life. "I have heard that he has become a well-known man," she said, "but I never understood what an important man he was till I went to that meeting."

There is another reflection about his home life which must occur to any visitor to the locality. Big houses and lovely grounds lay off the main road in the neighborhood, undoubtedly the homes of country gentlefolk. And one may venture to surmise their attitude toward this public firebrand who lives in their vicinity and used to be a village boy under the care of his uncle, the shoemaker. Is he on their visiting-list? I rather suspect not. The world must be turning topsy-turvy for them when they allow themselves to reflect, as they must at times, that this upstart has the entry to royal palaces and is one of the principal advisers of the King of England. I have an idea that something more potent than gall and wormwood is required to express their feelings. All this before the war. What can possibly be the attitude of mind of the local squires and lordlings now that this man has become an international statesman, probably the most forcible personality among that group of men who sit in conference to direct the activities and formulate the destinies of great European nations. Possibly I do them an injustice, and their habits of mind have changed of late.

During the big Budget fight Lloyd George, by virtue of his official position, had to attend occasional society functions. There was a duchess who could not avoid shaking hands with this person, who to her and her class was a monstrosity. After he had gone she spoke of the encounter to a friend with surprise in her voice. "I have just met Lloyd George," she said. "Do you know that he is really quite a nice man?" I have the impression that neither squires nor duchesses trouble Lloyd George very much, and that when this war is over and victory for his country secured he will go down to Criccieth and enjoy himself thoroughly in a golf-match with the local schoolmaster or one of the farmers of the district.

VIII

A CHAMPION OF WAR

The psychology of a community is as mysterious and subtle as that of an individual, and Lloyd George, despite all his so-called extravagance, all his depredations, and all his wounding words, was by way of being an acknowledged power in the country by the time the war with Germany burst out of the sky. The mysterious strength of the man worked on people against their will. Besides, there were tangible things which had to be faced. He had settled the great railway strike, he had passed several sweeping Acts of Parliament, he had brought into effect the iniquitous Budget, he had dismantled the British constitution by taking away the powers of the House of Lords. You may sneer at such a man, you may hate him, but you cannot ignore him. Sincere and religiously minded ladies used to write to the papers, wondering in all sincerity why Heaven permitted such a man to continue to live. A peer of the realm told his tenants that he would roast an ox whole for them in celebration of the day that Lloyd George went out of office, and, on top of this, the announcement that Lloyd George was going to speak drew together the unprecedented gathering of sixteen thousand people to hear him on a special day in the Midlands. You can sort out these varied facts to suit yourself, but taken altogether they convey a lesson. Let me add another point. Lloyd George, growing in influence, for years had been the special mark of attack for the *Daily Mail*, Lord Northcliffe's popular morning paper. When, after his House of Lords fight had been brought to a finish, Lloyd George set himself to a new colossal piece of legislation—namely, national health insurance—there was a concentrated attack by the *Daily Mail* to break the "poll tax" and Lloyd George with it. There had been a stream of violent criticism from the Northcliffe papers during the Budget days and the House of Lords battle, but the abuse was distributed pretty evenly upon the Government, though Lloyd George and Mr. Asquith got the major share. On this occasion all the guns were brought to bear on Lloyd George. The insurance tax was unpopular, and nothing that ridicule, covert insult, or open denunciation could achieve was left undone by the Northcliffe papers to smash Lloyd George and his policy. There was plenty of scope for attack. The Insurance Act was undoubtedly hurriedly conceived, and its complexities incompletely dovetailed. Whatever the merit of the conception, there had to be a score of rectifications when the measure came into operation. Some of Lloyd George's best friends complained of the injustices and irregularities of the Act. The *Daily Mail* was in the van of attack. To me it is surprising his assailants did not get Lloyd George down over this matter. They did not get him down. He carried the insurance bill, he forced it into operation, and he had left another milestone in his career behind him some time before the catastrophe of the European war appeared.

The country took a deep breath when the first shock of hostilities with Germany occurred, and then turned a passing attention to the British Cabinet, from which two or three members, including Lord Morley and Mr. John Burns, had resigned, presumably on account of their disapproval of the Government's action in going to war. Remarks came thick and fast as to the attitude of Ministers, and for a time it was suggested that Lloyd George was one of those who were on the verge of resignation. There was nothing impossible in the suggestion. A hater of wars, a fighter against wars all his life, he seemed just the kind of man to go adrift, and a good deal of movement was in readiness for the event. Special writers on the Conservative press sharpened their pencils assiduously for the announcement which could not be very long delayed. It must be remembered that Lloyd George in his earlier years had seemed to take a perverse delight in being on the unpopular side, and now to join what were called the "Pro-Germans" would really give him a chance for unpopularity such as he might never meet again.

He did not resign, and then the bigger men among his late opponents began to express the hope that in the conjunction of the parties now set up Lloyd George would come forward with his unexampled power over the democracy of Britain and stimulate them with trumpet note to the great effort that lay before them. I remember that Mr. Garvin, a doughty Conservative writer, came forward with a well-attuned appeal to Lloyd George to take the place which belonged to him as the leader of the common people of Britain. Little did he think that before many months were past Lloyd George would, by consent, be the leader of the whole nation, rich and poor alike.

For a week or two Lloyd George was quiet, and then it was announced that he would speak at a gathering in the Queen's Hall in the West End of London. A rush for tickets followed. I remember how crowded was the hall and how intensely silent was every soul when Lloyd George, wearing a gray summer suit with a black necktie, stepped to the front of the platform. There was none of the old, fierce, gay, fighting glitter about him. His mobile face was touched with gravity, his eyes were thoughtful, not provocative. He stood very erect, but his chin was drawn in a little, and his head canted forward. Responsibility lay on him, and every one could see it.

We all speculated on what he would say. Was he to make a half-and-half defense of the Cabinet war policy? Was he to try to explain why he had not resigned? He was always a master of the unexpected. What had he in store for us now? Speaking in the midst of a dramatic silence he said these words, slowly, almost conversationally: "There is no man who has always regarded the prospect of engaging in a great war with greater reluctance and greater repugnance than I have done through all my political life. There is no man more convinced that we could not have avoided it without national dishonor." That was the beginning of the most effective war speech since the start of hostilities. With scorn and logic and invective he raked the German position, and in a thrilling outburst invoked all that was honest, loyal, and strong in the British people to strike hard and deep on behalf of outraged Belgium. That was the first war speech of his life. The second was not long in following. It was made at the City Temple, a famous Nonconformist church in the heart of London. There it was that he said the same reason that made him a "Pro-Boer" made him an advocate of this war by Britain. He referred to the riotous Birmingham meeting. "It was a meeting convened to support exactly the same principle of opposition to the idea that great and powerful empires ought to have the right to crush small nationalities. We might have been right, we might have been wrong, but the principle that drove me to resist even our own country is the one that has brought me here tonight to support my country."

All through his life from boyhood onward Lloyd George had been a magnetic figure, one round whom action eddied in emergency. In any movement in which he was associated he automatically became the central personage, the individual looked to for inspiration and for motive power. Thus it was after his active entry into the patriotic campaign. The silent Kitchener at the War Office, the clear-headed Mr. Asquith at the head of the Government, were, by virtue of their positions, in the forefront, but within a week or two the newspapers and the public were calling attention to Lloyd George's services on behalf of the nation. His work as Chancellor of the Exchequer was indeed important; his personality made him even more important.

The shock of war had dislocated the financial system of the world and London, as the center of the financial system, was in the throes. Imagine Lloyd George as Finance Minister and the possibilities are obvious. Rapidly, drastically, and with his usual unexpectedness he began to act. His Budget with its tax on property had alienated from him the bankers and great financial houses, even where they were not previously prejudiced by their Conservative tendencies, and he had become anathema to them all. They had sneered at his originality, they had called him an ignorant person and spat out their contempt at him, but he had blithely brought them all to his will, whether they liked it or not, cheerfully throwing in a few words of warning and denunciation while he stripped them. Imagine, then, what he did in this crisis. He sent confidently to these old enemies of his, the leaders of the commercial and financial world, and said: "This country is thrown into financial chaos. I want the assistance of the best brains of expert people. I want you to give me your help as to the best way of putting things straight. I require that help at once. Will you come down immediately to 11 Downing Street and see me?" They went down to Downing Street. It was no time to hesitate. The arch-fiend might yet prove a savior. At Downing Street they found Lloyd George the most courteous man in high position they had ever met. He sat at their feet, so to speak. He listened attentively to all their opinions, and evolved from their various statements a true picture of the case. Then he took their suggested remedies one by one and quickly drew up schemes of relief—all the time with their co-operation and advice.

His quick mind pretty soon probed the length and depth of the situation. The firebrand and mob orator was, within a period of days, skilfully and delicately handling the tangled skein of national finance, winning golden opinions from his ancient opponents, not only by his mastery of technique, but also by the bold way he welded their views for new remedies.

Lloyd George went before the public and explained it all with a clearness and potency which made it apparent that money was as important as soldiers. It was in his first big speech on these lines that he coined the phrase "silver bullets" and made the nation understand that among his other operations was that of raising a huge war loan, to which every patriot must subscribe. "We need all our resources, not merely the men, but the cash. We have won with the 'silver bullet' before. We financed Europe in the greatest war we ever fought, and that is how we won." It was in this speech that he showed clearly the importance of giving British finance stability, and how that stability was threatened. A boy at school might have followed his explanation. "We have not only our own business to run; we are an essential part of the machinery that runs the whole international trade of the world. We provide capital and raise produce. We carry half the produce, not merely of our own country, but of the whole world. More than that, we provide the capital that moves that produce from one part of the world to another, not merely for ourselves, but for other countries. I ask every one to pick up just one little piece of paper, one bill of exchange, to find out what we are doing. Take the cotton trade of the world. Cotton is moved first of all from the plantation, say to the Mississippi, then down to New Orleans, then it is moved from there either to Great Britain or to Germany or elsewhere. Every movement is represented by a paper signed either here in London or in Manchester or Liverpool; one sender is practically responsible for the whole of these transactions. Not only that, but when the United States of America buys silk or tea from China, the payment is made through London. By means of these documents accepted in London New York pays for the tea bought in China. What has happened? All this fine, delicate paper machinery has been crashed into by a great war affecting more than half, and nearly two-thirds, of the whole population of the world. Confusion was inevitable. It was just as if one gave a violent kick to an ant-hill. The deadlock was not due to lack of credit in this country; it was due entirely to the fact that there was a failure of remittances from abroad. Take the whole of these bills of exchange. There were balances representing between 350,000,000 pounds and 500,000,000 pounds. There was that amount of paper out at that time with British signatures. Most of it had been discounted. The cash had been found at home from British sources, and failure was not due to the fact that Britain had not paid all her creditors abroad: it was due entirely to the fact that those abroad had not paid Great Britain."

That was the position as Lloyd George presented it, and the position with which he proceeded to deal, in a matter of hours, handling hundreds of millions with the confidence with which an enterprising tradesman handles dollars. A temporary moratorium for debts was established, balances were placed at the disposal of bankers, and guarantees given for the payment of bills accepted by British houses. There were other arrangements carried out equally swiftly. "An estimate of our national assets," said Lloyd George, in explanation of his action, "is 17,000,000,000 pounds. To allow the credit of the country to be put in doubt for twenty-four hours in respect of 350,000,000 pounds, most of it owing to our own people, would have been a criminal act of foolishness."

The financial houses cried blessings on Lloyd George's head. Even the *Daily Mail* gave him a careful word of praise. As for a great part of the country, it somehow got the impression that finance, under Lloyd George, was at least as important as military operations, and indeed the glowing speeches of the Chancellor of the Exchequer almost gave the impression that it was more important. When the Welsh statesman flung himself into an endeavor the business of the moment was to him the most important thing in all the world, and his own supreme belief made other people think so, too. By general consent Lloyd George did extremely well in his bold, rapid, and unconventional financial policy. He was, nevertheless, one of the first to realize that a new strong policy in directions other than finance was necessary if ultimate victory was to be achieved. Indeed, before the end of that fateful five months of 1914, during which a sturdy British army of less than two hundred thousand men had, under the pressure of the German hosts, been fighting a retreat, yard by yard and mile by mile, in a way which will live forever in British military history, there had been forced upon Lloyd George as one of the principal members of the Cabinet that there were grave deficiencies at the front in equipment, that the British soldiers, unsurpassable for valor, for their individual skill, and their contempt of death, were being, not only overwhelmed by German numbers, but swept down by gun-fire which was in extent and in power tremendously superior to that of the British. It was a deadening, horrible thought. All the fighting spirit of Lloyd George rose to meet the emergency. His financial arrangements were in train and going well. He was, it is true, Chancellor of the Exchequer, but he was also Lloyd George, and with the whole impetuosity of his nature he turned his attention to the needs of the British army in the field. His colleagues in the Cabinet were patriots and were able men, but they had not his lively imagination. Some of them had more technical knowledge, but their pedestrian processes of mind took very different channels from his lightning intuitions. I imagine sometimes that he was not very tactful. It is impossible to doubt that this was the time when he first became impatient with the methods of his chief, Mr. Asquith. It is equally impossible to doubt that at this time, also, he was moved sufficiently to challenge the policy of those in charge of the War Office, those on whose advice the Prime Minister naturally relied.

The existing methods were subsequently criticised as slow, conventional, unillumined by modern experiences. Our soldiers, it was said, were being swept out of action by an intensity and plenitude of new high-explosive shells, while we proceeded in the use of ordinary shells in ordinary quantities. We needed immensely greater numbers of shells, enormously improved shells, vast amounts of high explosive, new big guns, indeed a score of things, which were afterward obtained. Lloyd George at this period saw that, as usual, Britain was just "muddling through," relying on her stolidity and her power of endurance, rather than on her initiative and striking strength. His efforts to improve matters within Government circles could not have endeared him to his Government colleagues. But his blood was up, and he cared as little for their good opinion as he did for the good opinion of the squires and clergymen when he started professional life in Wales.

A movement was made to increase and better equipment, but it was slow and, in Lloyd George's view, it was ineffective. He fought on. At length he succeeded in impressing the seriousness of the situation on the Government, and it was just about this time that he became possessed of a powerful ally. The *Daily Mail*, in past years the most vindictive foe of Lloyd George, swung around to his support, took up the cry of insufficient shells, attacked Lord Kitchener, raised a scandal in the country. The *Times*, which now, like the *Daily Mail*, was under the proprietorship of Lord Northcliffe, joined in the fray. Extravagant and unjustifiable condemnation of Lord Kitchener shocked the public, but, at the same time, there was revealed an undoubtedly grave state of affairs in the insufficient provision of shells and explosives and other war material. A political upheaval followed. The Liberal Government was replaced by a Coalition Government, with Mr. Asquith still in command, but with Conservatives in the Ministry and with Lloyd George no longer Chancellor of the Exchequer, but Minister of Munitions, a new post created for him, that he might organize the country for the supply of needed war material for our soldiers at the front. At the same time started that informal, but effective, alliance between those sworn enemies of old, Lloyd George and Lord Northcliffe, an alliance between the two most powerful men of action in Britain in our generation.

IX

THE ALLIANCE WITH NORTHCLIFFE

I regard Lloyd George as the most interesting man in public life in Britain to-day. There is, however, another very interesting man in the country, though on a different plane from the Prime Minister. I mean Lord Northcliffe—the Alfred Harmsworth who started life for himself without help at seventeen, was a rich newspaper proprietor at thirty, and at forty was a national figure with wealth which would satisfy the wildest visions of any seeker after gold. He is about the same age as Lloyd George, and he has reached his zenith at about the same time. He is the principal owner, not only of the popular *Daily Mail*, but also of the famous *Times*, to say nothing of some forty other journals of various kinds. He is the inspiring spirit of all his publications, and I should think the papers which he controls convey their message, good, bad, or indifferent, to not less than six millions of people every day. The range of his influence is obvious, and though it is an influence primarily of the middle classes, it reacts upward and downward, and makes itself felt even on those who dislike his policies. Northcliffe is undoubtedly patriotic and is sincere, but he is, above all other things, a newspaper man. The huge circulations of his papers tell their story of his mind. He is a genius in knowing what will interest the common intelligence. He has labeled himself, sincerely enough, a Conservative in state affairs, though in his highly successful business he has never hesitated in trampling down conventions. I have to say this, moreover, that those who are brought into personal touch with Northcliffe, whether they agree with his opinions or not, find in him an appreciative employer, a generous-hearted friend, and a man always with big impulses. He is essentially a practical man. He has no dreams of improving the race, no gleaming visions of a community relieved of poverty and kindred ills.

Northcliffe was for years Lloyd George's most bitter public critic. He has now become his ally in the government of the British Empire. Despite the difference in their outlook on life, there are wonderful resemblances between the two men. There are sympathies, too. Northcliffe early recognized that Lloyd George was a person to be watched, not because of his speeches, but because he was a man of action and a man who got things done. On the other hand, Lloyd George, under cruel attacks, once said, reflectively: "What a power this man Northcliffe might be if he chose! He could carry through a political project while we were thinking about it. We talk of tackling the question of housing the poor people of this country. He could do it single-handed." To this a companion pointed out that he was asking too much of Northcliffe; he had not it in him.

What is this newspaper magnate like to look at? He is a heavy-shouldered man with a big, broad forehead, a massive jowl, and an aquiline nose. His wide mouth droops at the corners. In repose there is something of a scowl on his face, which is intensified in displeasure as his head shoots forward aggressively and almost wolfishly. And yet, on the other hand, in his pleasanter moments he has a boyishness and vivacity which are attractive. Nearly all who have been in his office, whether they are at present in his employ or not, will tell you he is a delightful man to work with. He will come into the reporters' room of the *Daily Mail*, sit on the edge of the table, smoke a cigarette, and talk to the men as if he were one of themselves. He likes them. They like him. Stories cluster round him. A young writer went out to investigate a series of happenings in a Midland town, was rather badly hoaxed, and was responsible for a good deal of ridicule directly against the paper. This is a deadly sin for a newspaper man, and the chiefs of the office were naturally severe about the matter. The writer in question, feeling that his career on the paper was over, went out of the office to lunch and, as bad luck would have it, encountered Northcliffe's automobile drawing up at the entrance. He knew "Alfred," as the proprietor is called, would be fuming, and was the last man on earth whom it was desirable to meet in such a mood. The young fellow braced himself for the attack as Northcliffe beckoned him forward. "What is this I hear? You have had your leg pulled, have you? Don't take it too much to heart. We all get deceived sometimes. I have had my leg pulled often before now. It's annoying, but don't worry about it."

He was frequently through the departments, making the acquaintance of new men, and exchanging a few sentences of conversation with the established members of the staff. Once he stopped at the desk of a junior sub-editor, whom he had not seen before, and said, "How long have you been with me?"

"About three months," was the reply.

"How are you getting on? Do you like the work? Do you find it easy to get into our ways?"

"I like it very much!"

"How much money are you getting?"

"Five pounds a week."

"Are you quite satisfied?"

"Perfectly satisfied, thank you."

"Well, you must remember this, that I want no one on my staff who is a perfectly satisfied man with a salary of five pounds a week."

A subordinate who had been a couple of years on the staff died as a result of an operation for appendicitis. He had a wife and one little child who were not very well provided for. On the day after the funeral, Northcliffe sent down and told her he had invested 1,000 pounds for her. Members of his staff who break down in health are sent for a prolonged rest on full salary, and, when necessary, are despatched abroad to recuperative climates with all their expenses paid. He is not, however, a man who suffers fools gladly, and those who come to him expecting, not only big salaries, but soft jobs, are quickly swept out in a cascade of hard words. He has a sense of humor. Once he turned the paper on to a search for an automobile which had run over a village child and then disappeared. He found it after a time, and it proved to be the car of his brother, Hildebrand, which, unknown to the owner, had been taken out for a joy ride by the chauffeur. There was something more than a chuckle among the other newspapers because Northcliffe in his enthusiasm had publicly offered 100 pounds reward for the discovery of the automobile and its owner. A few weeks later Fleet Street was busy trying to disentangle the mystery of the death of a young girl who had fallen from a railway carriage in a tunnel on the Brighton line. Various plans for the elucidation of the mystery were discussed between Northcliffe and the staff. In the course of the discussion some one made the suggestion:

"Why not offer a reward of 100 pounds for the discovery of evidence on the matter?"

"Yes," said Northcliffe, thoughtfully, "but where was my brother Hildebrand on that night?"

Deliberately placing behind him his previous attacks on Lloyd George, attacks personal and political, Northcliffe came out in strong support of the Minister of Munitions and plainly stated that it was only by revolutionizing the whole conduct of the war that victory could be assured within a reasonable time. There probably was no consultation between the two men. The support thus given to the Welshman was, in my opinion, perfectly genuine, and probably history will say it was a right and excellent course, though it involved stinging comment on Lloyd George's Cabinet associates, especially on Mr. Asquith and Lord Kitchener.

While this newspaper campaign was in progress Lloyd George set to work on his new effort, and that effort was the conversion of manufacturing Britain into a network of arsenals for the making of deadly implements of war. Again he made his special endeavor to appear as if they were the pivot of future victory. Forgotten for the time was finance. "Silver bullets" were no longer mentioned. "Shells, shells, shells!" was the cry of Lloyd George now, and the country echoed it. Enthusiastically he proceeded with his new task, and within a few days he had sketched a general scheme of operations, and within a few weeks the scheme was beginning to bear fruit. The difficulties were heavy, but he had this great advantage, that the country was prepared to do anything and to make any sacrifice which would lead toward victory. The established armament firms and the Government works had the task of providing shells and guns, and Lloyd George saw at a glance that this arrangement was tragically insufficient. To alter it he had to do many things. He had to secure the co-operation of manufacturers, especially the engineering firms who had been engaged in the ordinary occupations of peace time. He had to train new workmen, he had to enlist women, he had to persuade the trade-unions to remove their restrictions, he had to prevent the sale of alcohol in munition districts, he had to tell the capitalistic makers of munitions all over the country that they were only going to be left a percentage of their profits, and that the rest was going to be taken by the Government. This was part of his task. Many other things had to be attended to. There was, for instance, the matter of supply of steel from the foundries, and then, equally important, the question of transport by the railways. It would require a full book to tell of all the directions in which Lloyd George's efforts were expended in the ensuing weeks.

He went around the various big centers in the country and called together meetings of the prominent business men, particularly manufacturers, and suggested to them that they should form local committees which would schedule the locality for facilities in engineering work, and then outlined several ways in which they might act. They might first organize all the factories engaged in ordinary engineering work which could produce shells, or parts of shells, they might develop a big central factory in the district where central work could be done, and where finishing operations on partly made shells might be carried out. Everywhere he met cordial co-operation. Within a few weeks workshops previously used for making tramway metals, cranes, refrigerating apparatus, automobiles, overhead wires, agricultural implements, and many other kinds of material, were beginning to turn themselves into shell-factories under the direction of the local committees. Even watchmakers' shops were brought into use for some sections of work.

Meanwhile, Lloyd George initiated in every town and village of the country a census of metal-working lathes, so that no tool of this kind should be employed on needless work. Coincident with these operations, huge national shell-factories were planned for erection in various parts of the country. To co-operate the work of the local committees with headquarters in London a department of the Ministry of Munitions was set up in each big manufacturing center, and through this department Lloyd George kept in touch with all local operations.

Steps were taken to stimulate production by the recognized armament firms. It was six months after Lloyd George had taken control that I visited the Birmingham district, where I saw a new establishment for shell-work, a huge structure on the outskirts of the city planted where green grass was growing six months before, and under its one roof four thousand young women engaged in long lines at automatic lathes shell-making. This, as I said, was but one sample establishment. Hundreds of thousands of women were subsequently at the same work in various parts. The girls were drawn from all classes, and comprised school-teachers, domestic servants, shopgirls, stenographers, and the leisured daughters of the middle classes or of wealthy persons.

Lloyd George established in London, in connection with the Ministry of Munitions, a department of labor, to advise him on matters affecting workmen, a department of factory health which would tell him the best way of safeguarding the strength and efficiency of factory workers, an inventions department to encourage and examine inventions of all kinds which might be useful in war. He called in some of the leading business men of the country to help him in arranging, not only technical matters in the actual manufacture of shells and guns, but also the transportation of them, and the material of which they were made. He soon had around him in Whitehall a co-ordinated little army of iron and steel experts, explosive experts, railway experts, medical experts, and financial experts. They were the cream of business and professional intellect of the country. Under their driving stimulus shells and munitions began to pour out at an enormous rate. It was a cumulative production, and the high-water mark was not reached for many long months, but when it had been attained the production rate of shells by Germany was well beaten.

Lloyd George had no governmental red tape about his methods. For instance, he ordered a notice to be put up in each of the local munition offices, inviting callers who had inventions to submit them at once for sympathetic examination. Any one who went to the Ministry of Munitions in Whitehall and had real business could quickly see the Minister. He had no use for a halo of officialdom. A thousand difficulties rose to meet him as he built up the new organization, but he trampled them underfoot and went forward, heedless of whether he was making enemies or friends. An intermediate and important obstacle to his work was the fact that many of the trade-unions of the country had established rules which operated against an increase of production. These rules had been built up as protection against capitalists whose sole idea might be profits. It was necessary to sweep away these restrictions, and one of the arguments which Lloyd George used to the men was that he was not allowing employers to make fortunes out of the country's need, but was taking away all but a percentage of their new income and giving it to the Government. Even this was not sufficient in some cases to get all the workmen in the proper frame of mind. Lloyd George went down himself and addressed meetings of the men. Here is an extract from one of his speeches: "The enlisted workman cannot choose his locality of action. He cannot say, 'I am prepared to fight at Neuve Chapelle, but I won't fight at Festubert, and I am not going near the place called "Wipers."' He can't say, 'I have been in the trenches ten and a half hours, and the trade-unions won't let me work more than ten hours.' He can't say, 'You have not enough men here, and I have been doing the work of two men, and my trade-unions won't allow me to do more than my share.' When the house is on fire, questions of procedure and precedence and division of labor disappear. You can't say you are not liable to serve at three o'clock in the morning if the fire is proceeding. You can't choose the hour. You can't argue as to whose duty it is to carry the water-bucket and whose duty it is to put it into a crackling furnace. You must put the fire out. There is only one way to do it—that is, everything must give way to duty and good-fellowship, good-comradeship, and determination. You must put the whole of your strength into obtaining victory for your native land and for the liberties of the world."

The British trade-unions wanted but little persuading under such an appeal, and rights and privileges struggled for and won at heavy cost during half a century were cheerfully relinquished for the time being. There was some friction among small sections in connection with the powers taken by Lloyd George to punish workmen who struck work, or who dislocated operations in a workshop by leaving it to seek better money. But in the passion for victory which coursed through the veins of the nation the ruthless doings of Lloyd George were welcomed by the overwhelming majority of the community. He asked the English people to submit to shackles such as they had not known since the tyranny of the Middle Ages. They willingly and even enthusiastically agreed.

Lloyd George not only rushed the beginning of national shell-factories, since completed, but established large new towns of temporary houses in country districts with something more than the rapidity of camps on a rich gold strike. Britain, psychologically transformed, was in a large measure physically altered also.

And yet, when all was said and done, Lloyd George was not satisfied. He sought to stir the Cabinet to sterner work. The Cabinet was not by any means ineffective, but there was not enough driving force in it to please the Welshman. He wanted far wider and stronger measures taken in order to enlist the whole strength of the British people. Fiercely, day by day, the Northcliffe journals attacked Mr. Asquith, often with unfairness, and always did they exalt Lloyd George as the only man in the Cabinet who was really fit to lead. Then Lloyd George issued a column prognostication as the preface to a book, and it caused a great sensation. Here is what he said: "Nothing but our best and utmost can pull us through. If the nation hesitates when the need is clear to take the necessary steps to call forth its young manhood to defend honor and existence, if vital decisions are postponed until too late, if we neglect to make ready for all probable eventualities, if, in effect, we give ground for the accusation that we are slouching into disaster, as if we were walking along the paths of peace without an enemy in sight, then I can see no hope; but if we sacrifice all we own and all we like for our native land, if our preparations are characterized by grip, resolution, and prompt readiness in every sphere, then victory is assured."

This was a direct attack on the Cabinet, of which, of course, Lloyd George was a member. His words meant that the Government was proceeding along conventional paths, and not rising to great emergencies, and was lacking that desperate resolution so necessary in war. Thus it was that Lloyd George threw out to the world more than a hint of the difficulties he had had with different departments.

Northcliffe acclaimed this message heavens high. Some Liberals, on the other hand, began to see in Lloyd George an intriguer for the position of Prime Minister, and Lloyd George, not the first time in his life, throwing past prejudices and principles to the winds, came out as a strong supporter of conscription for the nation. Every young man must be serving his country either in the munition-factory or on the field of battle.

X

AT HIGH PRESSURE

The fundamental difficulty between Lloyd George and some of his colleagues was that he had ideas about running the country which were at variance with theirs. His Celtic temperament could not tolerate the slow muddling-through process, was impatient for daring new methods. He was disinclined for step-by-step procedure, and found reason for anger in the officials and Ministers who thought the war ought to be conducted according to book. There has yet to be told the full story, not only of all the obstacles which Lloyd George had to remove from his path in organizing the munition supply, but also of the hindrances which fettered the prosecution of the war as a whole with every ounce of strength, every shilling of money, at the disposal of the British nation.

I can imagine that Lloyd George was not a very pleasant colleague in the Cabinet during these intervening months. When the records come to be given it will be seen that he was constantly and furiously striking at the iron bars of custom and routine, that he was trying to turn the lip service of individuals to practical service. At times he reached the edge of desperate action.

It was in the thick of his other work that a crisis arose in South Wales, where the miners, numbering two hundred thousand, responsible for the supply of coal to the British navy, refused to work unless the employers conceded certain demands about pay and conditions. The seriousness of the position was appalling. The president of the Board of Trade, Mr. Runciman, struggled hard to bring about a settlement. He failed. Something had to be done and done at once. The country, looking around for a man to come to the rescue, fixed on Lloyd George. He left the Ministry of Munitions in Whitehall, took a train down to South Wales, had a straight talk with the employers, another straight talk with the men, and in one day settled affairs and got the men to continue their work. I cite this as a passing illustration of how Lloyd George was Britain's man-of-all-work, and of how the nation had to turn to him practically every time it was in difficulty.

While struggling to speed up the Cabinet on a hundred matters Lloyd George became impressed with the necessity of increasing the size of the British army, already millions strong. The voluntary system had hitherto been relied on, and there was strong opposition, both in the Cabinet and in the country, to tentative proposals for conscription. Lloyd George took an early opportunity of showing that he was on the side of the conscriptionists. There was an outburst of protests, but it proved of no avail, and it was largely through Lloyd George that conscription in Britain became an established fact. Even then he was by no means satisfied with the way affairs were being handled, and the newspapers were speculating on his next big attempt, when tragedy descended on the country in the unexpected death of Lord Kitchener by the sinking of the war-ship *Hampshire* off the coast of Scotland. Kitchener had been Minister for War.

Who was to be the new man? There was really only one man in the running, and Lloyd George forsook his munition work, now practically accomplished, and went over to take charge of the War Office. Coincident with his acceptance of this post new arrangements in the organization were made, and it was no doubt largely by his influence that General Sir William Robertson was installed at Whitehall as Chief of Staff, virtually commander-in-chief of the British armies. He was a man after Lloyd George's own heart, a soldier who had risen from the ranks, a quiet man who would stand no nonsense, and one who knew modern war conditions from A to Z.

Here, then, began a new phase of the European conflict. From the shops, offices, farms, and factories of Britain there had sprung up an amateur army, millions strong, and the organization of this new national force was under the supervision and control of a Minister who began life as a village boy in a cottage of a shoemaker, and under the military direction of a commander-in-chief who also sprang from the common people, and as a young man was an ordinary trooper in the ranks. It could never henceforth be said that Britain, the most aristocratic country on earth, had not been content to hand over the reins to democracy in the greatest emergency of her history. Robertson and Lloyd George worked well together, and there can be no doubt that under their joint effects the British forces in the field attained a fighting value which was not excelled by any other army in existence on either side in the great conflict.

Frequently Lloyd George was in the trenches at the front. From time to time he was deep in consultation in Paris or at home with the leading statesmen and commanders of France, Italy, and Russia. All this was only a few months ago. I saw him in the House of Commons at the time. The strain was undoubtedly telling on him, but was not oppressing him. His hair was a little whiter, his face was pallid, and thinner than of yore, but his eyes were like burning coals. He had much to bear apart from the actual work, for there were large sections of politicians and several influential newspapers who openly said that ambition was his curse, that he was undermining Mr. Asquith who had been his greatest political friend, and that all his discontent was directed toward an ultimate dramatic stroke which would make him Prime Minister. Many of the Liberals who used almost to worship him made no secret of the fact that he had lost their allegiance, while the extreme Socialists denounced him as a traitor to the working classes, inasmuch as he was tyrannizing over them by his war measures. Moreover, many of his opponents in the Cabinet must have regarded him with some feeling of distrust. He said no word in defense of Mr. Asquith, whom the Northcliffe press persistently and violently assailed. The conclusion is inevitable that Lloyd George shared some of the opinions then expressed. Taking Lloyd George's nature into account, the situation may be imagined, and it was not hard to see that a climax must come sooner or later.

It was approaching swiftly. Meanwhile the transformation of Britain in which Lloyd George had had so large a hand was proceeding. No longer could it be said that the old country was lethargic. In all directions was the elementary strength of this stolid people manifesting itself. Classes were uniting in the determination that there should be limitless spending of energy, of blood, and of treasure, that the harder grew the fight the stronger should be the will, the livelier the action, till the great danger was trodden finally underfoot. For months past it could have been said:

All the youth of England are on fire
And silken dalliance in the wardrobe lies.

Now most of the people had reached the decision that nothing but extermination should lead to their defeat.

And leave your England as dead midnight still,
Guarded with grandsires, babies, and old women,
Either past or not arrived to pith and puissance,
For who is he whose chin is but enrich'd
With one appearing hair that will not follow
Those cull'd and choice-drawn cavaliers to France?

It was really a very-much-alive England, though strangely changed, which the amateur fighters had left behind them on their departure for the field of war. Tens of thousands of women unaccustomed to hard labor were tiring their bodies from early morning till night so that there would be more men for the fighting-line. The state had virtual possession of the great industries, of engineering, of railway transportation, and of shipping. The liquor trade had been cut down to narrow limits which, while it benefited the health and efficiency of the population, ruined financially a great many property-owners. The trade-unions had relinquished their rights, so that every hour of the day and night there should be no strong and healthy arm which was not lending aid to the country in its need. Every man in the country up to the age of forty was either in the army or doing some useful war work at home.

Steps had been taken to prevent the price of coal being raised to consumers, and this was shortly to be followed by the Government acquisition of the whole of the South Wales coal-field. Already a movement was afoot to regulate the food-supply and to restrict expensive luxuries. At the head of these tremendous changes was Lloyd George, whose so-called socialistic legislation a few years before had roused spasms of rage among classes which now belauded his every action and announced him as the coming savior of his country. If there is any consistency in human nature at all, it is hardly possible that there were not those who recalled his incendiary speeches, his unsparing legislative action of the Budget days. And yet there were no complaints. Millionaires placed their money at his disposal. The dukes paid him homage. All the while Lloyd George grew harder in the face. Big changes were still necessary if the war was to be brought to an end victoriously and rapidly.

I have indicated the Minister for War as the moving spirit in all those changes of that tangled period, but he was only a single member of the Ministry which set them in motion, although there could be no doubt in the mind of any one really acquainted with public affairs in Britain at this time that his was the driving force behind the reforms, that they were largely forced on by his resistless spirit, even as he was desirous to push them further and quicken the pace. Meanwhile in France, in Italy, and in Russia Lloyd George's name roused enthusiasm wherever it was mentioned. News from America indicated that he was well known and much talked of there. In the Scandinavian capitals which I visited toward the close of 1916 I found that it was Lloyd George whom the statesmen, the professors, the business men, and the common people were eager to hear about above all others. In Germany he was hated and feared more than any other British statesman.

XI

HIS INCONSISTENCIES

According to all the rules which are supposed to guide the rise of a self-made man, Lloyd George should have been a master of routine, with the orderly mind and undeviating habits without which we are sometimes told no person of affairs can secure permanent success. It is much to be regretted that Lloyd George lends no aid to the well-established maxims. The teachers and preachers who seek to implant in the young the principles of continuousness of purpose and of regularity and of kindred qualities must turn their backs on Lloyd George. They will find nothing from him to go into the text-books, for in the course of his career the Welsh statesman has trampled on every sound rule for securing success. That a man with so many contradictions in him should have ever maintained his upward course is not encouraging to the formalists, though it is very interesting to ordinary people.

There never was a man who could more quickly master the intricacies of a business problem, and yet from his very early days he was quite unbusiness-like in many things. He laughingly says that as a young lawyer down in Wales he showed serious incapacity in his profession, at least in one respect: "I never sent in any bill of costs. The result was I never had any money." Later when his brother, three years younger than himself, joined him in partnership matters improved. "The firm did not then suffer from this serious professional drawback," explained Lloyd George. He is an adept at phrases, and yet all through his life he has hated writing. There is a tradition among some of his friends that even in his less busy periods, if you wanted to get a reply from him on any topic you had to send him two postcards addressed to yourself, on one of which was written, "Yes," and on the other, "No." This, it was said, was the only way you could make sure of a prompt response, or indeed of any response at all. He has been the supreme business organizer of Britain during the war—in finance, in industrial operations, and latterly in actual army work—and in each direction he has sketched out and carried into effect an intensive efficiency which it is not too much to describe as the admiration of the world, yet all the time his office day-by-day arrangements would certainly shock the ordinary merchant or banker. He makes contingent appointments and forgets all about them. Some incidental scheme adopted by him on a Saturday is on Monday thrust into limbo by the pressure of other schemes. If he were to schedule his office day into five-minute appointments he would still be unable to see only a proportion of the important men and executive chiefs who desire to get in touch with him, and yet he will allow himself to be drawn into an hour's keen discussion with persons who have some minor topic which appeals to him. Withal, he gets things done. Some intuition, some instinct for right action, takes him to his goal. The task in hand is always accomplished to the limit of efficiency. You may seek his secret in vain. Probably part of it lies in his natural power of selecting his instruments. All the same I do not envy the lot of his two principal private men secretaries and the girl stenographer whose business it is to follow and, to some extent, direct his erratic course throughout his office hours.

His speeches which in their printed form sell literally by the million, are scarcely prepared at all before he gets on the platform. Sometimes the wording as it appears in cold black and white lacks a little polish, but it has a vital and stimulating force marking it out as distinctive literature. He has a few notes as to facts and figures and weaves them into a picture as he stands before his audience. When his famous speech at Limehouse thrilled England a London newspaper proprietor went down to see him in the House of Commons. "Why didn't you let me know you were going to make that speech?" he said. "I would have had special arrangements made for reporting it and describing it." "There was nothing special in it," said Lloyd George, in genuine surprise. "It was just an ordinary talk about the Budget. I went down to Limehouse and spoke to an audience I found there, that's all."

No one will deny Lloyd George's courage. On a hundred stricken fields he has shown it. Yet he confesses to a timorousness and nervousness whenever he is waiting on a public platform with a speech ahead of him. This proven, stern man of action is just a trembling bunch of nerves, afraid of the people in front of him, afraid of the people by his side on the platform, as he sits waiting the fateful second when the chairman shall announce his name.

Lloyd George's unexpectedness comes from the fact that he is a many-sided man. Success has not atrophied either his manners or his impulses. He is not ashamed to be very human because he has become very important. I remember how, during the stress of the Budget fight, when, if ever, he was at a tension, he went off for a week-end with the Attorney-General and a distinguished journalist. They had a railway compartment to themselves on the journey from London. Part of the time was passed in singing popular songs, the choruses of which Lloyd George trilled out enthusiastically. And yet Lloyd George is not a stranger to the formalities. High office brought to him a marked care for those little chivalries which are part of Parliamentary warfare. In the height of the fight fatigue sometimes overwhelmed even his sturdy frame and spirit, and he would snatch half an hour's respite from the Treasury bench in his own room behind the Speaker's chair. But he would break off this short indulgence instantly when the ticker indicated that his principal opponents had begun to speak. Directly it was shown that Mr. Austen Chamberlain, Mr. Balfour, or some other leader was on his feet Lloyd George would hurry into the chamber to listen, even though he might know perfectly well that they had nothing to say that mattered at the moment. He regarded it as important to pay them the courtesy of listening to any speech they made, however casual or trivial.

One of the charges against Lloyd George during his public life has been his inaccuracy in small things, his disregard of detail, and in some ways this is a justifiable charge. And yet the man has a perfect passion for detail when he is aroused and when he believes detail necessary. In instituting the Department of Munitions he made himself in the course of only a week or two a real expert in the hundred intricacies connected with the manufacture of shells. Short of handling the steel himself I doubt if there was any man in the country, who knew more about the nature of all the deadly missiles, from the small rifle bullet up to the great shell which weighs a ton and travels some fifteen miles. Delicate chemical processes connected with high explosives rapidly became an open book to him. As new discoveries were made incidental difficulties connected with the filling of shells occupied the concentered study of the manufacturers. Lloyd George plunged into the new arrangements. One morning he had an appointment in London with a group of half a dozen munition-makers from the north of England and the Midlands for the purpose of investigating some special difficulties in a new process. The matter was one of importance as well as of difficulty. Point by point was taken and lunch-time arrived without a complete elucidation. Lloyd George swept aside all other appointments for the day. The thing had got to be mastered. He took the six experts out with him to lunch and went on with the discussion over the meal. He brought them back to the Munition Department afterward and he went on with the matter all the afternoon. Tea was served, and still he would not let his advisers escape. It was nearly dinner-time before the difficulties were conquered and the tired experts were permitted to go. Lloyd George, cheered by the achievement, had a little food, and then proceeded to work far into the night to clear up some of the arrears of the day's routine. As for the staff, they had to work, too. There are no easy times for those associated with Lloyd George when he is under pressure.

These are examples from recent times, but throughout the whole of his career there have been contradictions which have staggered friends as well as enemies. I do not believe there is a more sincere man in public life; there certainly is no shrewder one, and yet when he was Chancellor of the Exchequer in charge of the finances of the country he was imprudent enough in an impulsive moment to invest privately some hundreds of pounds in a commercial company, an investment perfectly innocent in itself, but one which a worldly-wise person would have realized must lay open to attack any Chancellor of the Exchequer who had enemies. He never gave the thing a thought. He had always been a comparatively poor man. He saw a good investment and he put some of his savings into it. His opponents became aware of the matter, and in storms of virtuous passion held him up to execration as a corrupt politician who was using his position to make himself rich. There were bursts of unholy joy among the Conservatives. That innocent investment in Marconi shares was perhaps the most stupid thing in Lloyd George's public life. He gave his explanation with vigor and clearness, but, nevertheless, I fancy he must have kicked himself privately about the whole thing. Notwithstanding, however, the disadvantage at which he had placed himself, opponents found that now, as on other occasions, it was not a pleasant exercise to attack the Welshman. He had a horrid habit of defending himself by hitting back, and he usually hit very much harder than his attackers were capable of doing. When the dukes and earls fell on him in all their noble rage and dignity he culled stories from the past about them. One of the attacks on him was by Earl Selborne, who had been a Cabinet Minister in a Conservative administration. Lloyd George permitted himself no false delicacy about the noble earl. "He contends there is no correspondence between his story and mine. He is quite right. I have already pointed out the essential difference. I bought shares in a company which had no contract with the Government, and my purchase of even these shares was subsequent to the acceptance of the wireless tender by the Government. Earl Selborne was a director of a company during the time it was initiating and acquiring a huge contract with the Government, of which he was a member. His story is, therefore, not mine."

There had probably never been a politician in British public life who was so affectionately regarded by all those persons who were brought into personal contact with him, whether they agreed with him or not. Pressmen whose duty it was to berate him in the papers were generally fond of him personally. Opponents in the House of Commons when not engaged in combat had, in most cases, an active liking for him. Business men and persons not connected with politics after once meeting him had nothing but good to say of the "Welsh demagogue." And in face of all this Lloyd George has truly been the most hated man of his generation. He used to chuckle over it—which sent his opponents to the last degree of fury. "The dukes," he would remark, cheerily, "are scolding like omnibus-drivers, and the lords swearing like stable-boys." He would fling out his hand with a humorously despairing gesture about it.

Lloyd George was not very precise in his attacks sometimes. Though he was very rarely, perhaps never, successfully challenged on the general basis of his charges, his vivid wording always brought on him a flood of recriminations. He was called an "ignorant demagogue," an "unscrupulous electioneer," was accused of using "false sentiment" and of "setting class against class." His principal weapons throughout, it was said, were his inaccuracies and offensive personalities. The exasperated Conservatives, only a few months before the war, secured the time of the House of Commons to indict him for some of these sins. Here was the resolution moved from the Conservative benches: "That this House contemplates with regret the repeated inaccuracies of the Chancellor of the Exchequer and his gross and unfounded charges upon individuals." No motion could have pleased Lloyd George better. Ponderous and dignified were the speeches against him. He replied with a quizzical lightness, and did not refrain from personal remarks even in the course of his defense. He demonstrated the general accuracy of his speeches, ridiculed the indictment against himself, and showed how it arose partly from political prejudices, partly from the mental obtuseness and anger of his opponents. A portion of his speech recalled the things the Conservatives attacking him said about Joseph Chamberlain, now one of their idols. They were remarks made during Chamberlain's radical days.

"One Tory Minister said he spoke 'with customary inaccuracy.' Another Minister talked about 'his habitual incapacity for being accurate.' Another said he was 'setting class against class.' The *Times*, using the language of the gentleman in opposition to-night, said he was 'forgetting what was due to his dignity and responsibility as a Cabinet Minister.' He was compared by the leader of the

House to 'Jack Cade.' Another called him 'an unscrupulous demagogue.' Another said he was 'weeping crocodile tears for electioneering purposes.' I seem to recognize some of these epithets. I am amazed at the lack of imagination in the vituperation of honorable men opposite." When the laughter and cheering had died away Lloyd George said that Chamberlain was fifty at the time these things were uttered, the age at which he himself stood. "So there is hope for me," he said. It is difficult to tackle a man like that.

No one would deny that Lloyd George has gone back on many of the opinions he used to hold so firmly. The exhilarating names he called members of the House of Lords have been replaced by invitations to some of them to join him as Ministers in a Cabinet of which he is the head. No doubt he would give good reasons for the change, but the fact remains. His mobile mind is ever adapting itself to what he considers the exigencies of the times, though no one could with less justice be named a time-server. "Other times, other means, other manners" may be described as his attitude of mind. If at the moment the welfare of the community in his judgment demanded certain courses of action no words of his in the past, no principles that he had held, would prevent him from adapting himself or from using whatever powers lay to his hand. As motive forces in social life are almost invariably to be obtained from individuals, Lloyd George without shame and without hesitation has proceeded to use individualities wherever he found them suitable for his purpose. Meanwhile the worshiper of consistency can find in him no idol.

The crowning inconsistency of Lloyd George's career I have not yet described. So far as he owed success in life to any man except himself he owed it to Mr. Asquith, the Prime Minister. Lloyd George has all the sensitiveness and affection of the Celtic nature, and must certainly have had within him a well of gratitude to this man who had been so great a friend to him. Yet it came about that he eventually decided it was his duty to pull this man from the throne and take his place there.

XII

HOW HE BECAME PRIME MINISTER

In some lights it seems rather a shabby thing that Lloyd George should have ousted Mr. Asquith and taken his place as Prime Minister. Mr. Asquith, with great intellectual attainments and with the highest attributes of an English gentleman, had been at the head of the British Government for eight years, and during this period big achievements had been inscribed on Britain's story. He had been a strong and constant friend of Lloyd George who, under his leadership, had risen from the position of a minor Minister to giant eminence. Then at a crucial moment Lloyd George overthrew him. Stated baldly like that, the thing doesn't read very well. I believe there are some leaders in England who will never forgive Lloyd George. It remains to be said that they are taking a narrow and immediate view of a drama so immense that its proper perspective will only be available many years hence. They are trying to test men's souls under strain in a small mechanical balance. Forces were at work such as are only met with once or twice in centuries. You cannot bring a puny, every-day judgment to bear on issues which may mean misery or happiness to millions of people, and life or death to a great proportion of them. In such circumstances the raw strength of big men comes out, and the spectacle is not always pleasant to the gentle-minded.

I am not one of those who believe that Lloyd George sordidly schemed to become Prime Minister, though I am sure that in some side reflections from time to time he realized quite certainly that one day he would be Prime Minister of his country. I believe that from the moment he decided the war was a right one and must be pressed to victory he concentrated the whole of his heart and soul, all of his bewildering and compelling properties, to the task of securing victory. And that the remarkable success he attained, first in the sphere of finance, then in the provision of munitions, thirdly in the raising of armies and general organization for battle, led him quickly to a vision of the whole contest, a vision unshared by his colleagues, but of dazzling clearness to himself.

His whole being, designed for the emergencies of combat, quivered and thrilled as he saw the hundred directions in which urgency and rapidity and ruthlessness could forge the weapons of success. I believe he was completely selfless about the matter. He made efforts to touch various spheres of war organization with the white-hot spirit which possessed himself, and became partly the terror, partly the admiration, of those among whom he moved. And then, realizing more and more, week by week, what he regarded as the inertia in the departments that ran the country, and seeing the importance of stirring the feelings of his principal Cabinet colleagues to wholesale, passionate, fear-nothing strokes which should bring the end of the war within sight, there grew upon him resistlessly the thought that he must himself secure supreme control of the war in Britain. I believe the idea took hold of him, not from any vulgar motive, but in the way that religion grows upon a man, possessing him utterly, leaving him heedless of the criticism directed against his personal aims.

What was the system he was up against? In the British Cabinet each Minister is the head of his own department, and in normal times the Prime Minister doesn't interfere in the departments, although, as chairman of the Cabinet, his consent has to be given to any big national policy initiated by another Minister. Mr. Asquith had strong and clever men around him, and, quite apart from the fact that he was the most chivalrous of chiefs, he trusted their capacity. Strong and capable as they were, they had not the flashing genius of Lloyd George, certainly had not his genius for war, implying large decisions and great risks. They plodded along and threshed out plans and put some of them into execution. To Lloyd George both the plans and the way they were carried out were half-hearted. To him there was always delay, never the stark action which he believed was everywhere necessary. Decisions were taken too late and were not carried out with promptitude or thoroughness.

For months Lloyd George was in a state of simmering revolt. He received support from powerful organs in the press, notably from the *Times* and *Daily Mail*. The tone of their criticism is best summarized in the suggestion that Mr. Asquith was "an amiable old gentleman," unfitted for the position of leader of a nation at war for its life. Far less than justice was accorded him, but under the stress of war the most stolid people became impatient, and there was undoubtedly manifested in many sections of the public a desire for more strenuous leadership. The difficulties with which Mr. Asquith had had to contend were certainly not fully appreciated, though they will be later on. He was the head of a Coalition Government, and had kept that Government together with a managing skill to which everybody paid tribute. The claim of the Lloyd George supporters was that qualities different from those required for the skilful handling of a Government were necessary in a war Prime Minister. It looks as if Lloyd George shared this opinion. He came to the conclusion that he must make his stroke. One fateful day he presented to Mr. Asquith an ultimatum to the effect that the conduct of the war should be placed in the hands of a small committee of three or four members who should have absolute power, and that Mr. Asquith himself should not be on it, or, if so, should be a member in name only.

Mr. Asquith tried to get him to compromise. Lloyd George would have none of it. If Mr. Asquith would not agree he would resign, he said, and he was supported by the Conservative members of the Government. Mr. Asquith and his supporters would not give way. There were one or two exciting days of secret negotiations, and then, a deadlock being reached, there was but one course to be pursued, and that was for the entire Cabinet to place its resignation in the hands of the King. It must have been a bitter moment for Mr. Asquith. Indeed, it was probably an unhappy time for Lloyd George. Nevertheless, he flinched not.

The whole Cabinet went out of office. The King, who is bound by precedent, sent for the leader of the Conservatives, Mr. Bonar Law, and offered him the position of Prime Minister and the task of forming a Government. Owing to the split-up of the parties and the various cross-currents, Mr. Law felt himself unable to carry out the formal request of the King. Then the expected happened, and the King sent for Lloyd George, who promptly expressed his willingness to try to form a Government, so long as he was assisted in the task by Mr. Bonar Law. He was successful. His Cabinet, rapidly brought into being, consisted of several Labor men, several Conservatives, some notable members of the House of Lords, and also, quite a novel feature, some captains of industry, whom Lloyd George took from their private businesses to run the business departments of the state. A war council was formed, consisting of Lloyd George himself; Mr. Arthur Henderson, the leader of the Labor movement; Lord Curzon, and Lord Milner. (The most recent claims to distinction of the latter two was their violent opposition to Lloyd George's Budget and the Parliament bill.) The sum total of arrangements was that the new Prime Minister became virtually a dictator. He rules England to-day.

What will be his record as Prime Minister? It may be taken as a certainty that his tenure of office will be a memorable chapter in English history. That he will use to the utmost his natural powers in bringing the war to a conclusion satisfactory to his country goes without saying. I am inclined to think that there is no one who yet realizes the lengths to which he will go in order to secure victory. No precedent will stand in his way, no consideration of popularity or unpopularity will deter him. That he may break himself in his attempt is a trifle to him. I do not think he will break himself, for he has reserves not usually found in a single personality. Obloquy may again take the place of the praise which now encircles him. He may yet be assailed by some of the new colleagues whom he has chosen, and the newspapers which have supported him may turn against him. But if he lives and preserves his health he will win the war. He is not entirely admirable, but nothing will obliterate his powers of success but extinction.

He has the imagination to envisage the uncountable forces at his disposal in the British Empire, and if need be he will use these forces to their very limits. Already he has proceeded on new lines. With that intense practicalness which goes with his spiritual exaltation he has appointed a grocer and a provision-dealer to control the food-supplies of the country, has put a ship-owner at the head of the mercantile marine, has given to a man who was a working steel-smelter the unshackled control of labor, has chosen as another Cabinet Minister a young American who has made a fortune in business—staggering appointments indeed for conservative old England. But that is only a beginning. The Prime Minister has hitherto been but the titular head of the various departments of his Government, but now he is going to be the real head, for Lloyd George has set up a Prime Minister's Department which co-ordinates continually all the various Government offices. Lloyd George means to be no mere figure of dignity as a Prime Minister.

What more can he do? There is no end to the war expedients which are to his hand if the conflict with Germany goes on. If more young men are wanted for the army I can see him levying the whole of the women in the country for work on the farms and in the offices or its shops. He may turn his eyes to the overseas dominions, where there are scores of millions of population from which separate vast new armies may be drawn. I have little doubt that erelong the enemies of Britain will come up against the quality of unexpectedness which has so often discouraged his opponents at home. No field of endeavor will be closed to him. I can even see him with a board of inventors and constructors setting to work to provide, let us say, a fleet of one hundred thousand aeroplanes which shall, in truth, make the invasion of Germany possible. There are other novel fields of effort with potentialities of equal or even greater scope.

It was complained of Mr. Asquith that he was too much of a gentleman, too kindly and considerate even to those who harassed him, that he feared to repress those who strove to make his tenure of office impossible. There will not be any nonsense of that kind about Lloyd George. Heaven help those who, however highly placed and whatever their services to him in the past, now stand in his way. Interesting suggestions have been made that his recent alliance with Northcliffe was a fatal mistake for him, because Northcliffe, in pursuit of newspaper sensations, combined with patriotic aims, having helped to place him in the seat of power, will presently turn on him without scruple and without mercy. Well, there may even be an attempt in that direction. I know both men pretty thoroughly, having been brought into personal contact with each, and watched the work and studied the power of both of them for years. If Northcliffe attempts any action of the kind indicated he will find that he has gone out for a walk with a tiger. He has no dignified Mr. Asquith to deal with now. If Northcliffe, by any journalistic sensations, interferes in what in Lloyd George's opinion is the proper and efficient conduct of the war, Lloyd George will break him like a twig and without a second thought. Some people of Britain talk of what will happen to Lloyd George when Northcliffe throws him over. One can only smile. To stop the publication of the *Daily Mail* and the *Times*, wrecking a million pounds' worth of private property at least, and ruining Northcliffe on the way, will be twenty minutes' cheery work for Lloyd George in his present mood, if he thinks the interests of Britain demand it.

It will be found from now until the treaty of peace is signed that Lloyd George will be the personal director of democratic Britain, as grim an autocrat as was Oliver Cromwell, and when the plenipotentiaries meet around a table to settle terms there will be among them the blue-eyed Welshman, pleasant of manners and with iron will, putting in some commas and taking out the clauses he doesn't like.

XIII

THE FUTURE OF LLOYD GEORGE

When this war is concluded there must be a new era for the world. Already there are signs of its approach. Generations hence there may again be awful conflicts between nations, spasms of hell in which the blood and anguish of millions will pay their tribute to the beast in man, but it will not be in our time, and in the interval, the beginning of which must be upon us very quickly, a new order of things will arise among the civilized people of the globe. Stricken humanity will insist on happier prospects for its children and its children's children. In the formulation of that new order of things I can see Lloyd George as one of the main instruments.

In the first place, Britain will be a revivified country after the war, chastened in some ways, teeming with new thoughts, pulsing with a new virility for at least a generation. Class prejudice will be lessened, perhaps in some directions will be completely wiped out. There will probably be a centralized effort after the trials which all the people have suffered together to reconstruct the social fabric so that all the people of the country, with the exception of those who are lazy or criminal, shall have the means by which they may be able to secure a decent livelihood and need have no fear of poverty-stricken old age. I foresee the disintegration of the older political parties and the building up of new ones, in which the great contending features will be the means and methods by which the new Britain shall be established. The old party shibboleths will be swept away. Mere words and windy generalities will be displaced from influence and the nation's leaders will deal with facts.

The education of the war has brought everybody in the country up against hard realities. While prejudices and so-called principles have been put in the background, there has been going on a learning of new lessons. Lloyd George will undoubtedly be the main figure in the building up of the national edifice. The war will effect political changes which a generation of Parliamentary efforts could not have brought about. Hundreds of thousands of men drawn from shops, factories, offices, who have been hardened and stimulated by their out-of-doors campaigning, will be averse from returning to their old drab conditions, and coincident with this the rich and beautiful farmlands of England will be made available in holdings for such as wish to settle on the land and to establish themselves there. Cottage dwellings and farm buildings will be put up by the thousand with the assistance of the state. The settlers from the towns will not only find health for themselves and families, but by their activities will add enormously to the food-supplies of the country through their market gardens, their dairy farms, as well as by the extra corn which will be produced by them.

Lloyd George's heart and soul will be in this project, for, country born and bred as he is, he knows not only the troubles, but also the opportunities and the personal joys of the population on the land. I regard a revolution on these lines in England as a practical certainty. It may be asked, Where is the money to come from for all this? The answer is, that loans from the state are inevitable, but they will be remunerative loans which presently will yield returns, not only in the shape of interest, but in new food-supplies and also, not less important, in the benefits of new physical strength and new happiness in life to big sections of the population. Sacrifices will be asked for from the great land-owners, but they will be sacrifices of sentiment rather than of money, because these proprietors will certainly be well recompensed financially for any land that is taken from them.

But this transformation in the countryside will be only one phase of the new Britain. Virtual revolution is certain in town life—and something like forty millions out of the fifty millions of population have their present homes in towns and cities, and not in the country. A great stimulation of production may be looked for under the lessons of war-time. Scores of inventions have been devised under the strain of the war's demands and the discoveries in chemistry, in mechanics, and in other directions will remodel certain industries and create fresh ones. Novel methods of organization have been brought into use and have greatly aided efficiency, but even these developments will be but supplementary to the changes in the methods of British industrial life. The Labor movement of Britain, which has obtained during the war a political power previously unknown in British Government, has altered its modes of procedure, subordinated its laws, and generally transfigured itself. The position can never be readjusted to the old basis. This will carry with it remarkable results. Something like three million trade-unionists constitute the effective Labor movement of Britain, and the unions, with their rights and privileges, have only been built up by half a century of struggle against prejudice, against material interests, against opposition in Parliament. In the last ten years, however, enormous progress has been made. Forty Labor men have seats in the legislature, and the combination of trade-union rules and regulations safeguarding workmen and restricting employers has become as effective as a legal charter. Hours and conditions of labor as well as wage rates in the various trades have been set up and continually strengthened with a view to prevent exploitation by employers, and though there is necessarily a running struggle with regard to isolated matters, there has come to exist, on the whole, amicable relations between the great unions, on the one side, and the great employers, on the other. Under Lloyd George's appeals during the war trade-unions have flung overboard the restrictions they had imposed, have permitted unskilled people to come in and do parts of their work, permitted women to take a hand, allowed employers to increase hours of work, and voluntarily have taken upon themselves the old burdens which they had fought so long to shake off. They have had at least this recompense that, so far as money is concerned, they have not been badly off. In important industries, notably in munition-making, piece-work—payment according to work accomplished—is the rule, with the result that large sums are earned by those who choose to work hard and to work early and late. The general result of all this has been a marvelously accelerated output of material as compared with that which would have been produced under old conditions. The unions have the promise of the Government that all their old rules shall be restored after the war if they want them. It has become inconceivable that incidental advantage secured in these abnormal times shall be thrown away when peace comes just because of a traditional adherence to principle. Employers, also, seeing the tremendously increased results, will be eager to maintain the new acceleration. Are the unions, for the sake of old prejudices, to put back the clock and throw out all the employment of the women who have entered the hitherto-reserved industries, and to abolish the overtime work? Are they, moreover, to return to the old principles of prohibiting an operative from doing more than a certain amount of work in a certain time—a practice quite defensible so far as it arose from the greed of employers who, with their men on piece-work, finding the rate of production increased, promptly put back the rate of payment so that workpeople should never earn more than a certain amount by day or by week? Is there to be a reaction in all these directions? There is not. Unions will not want all their old provisions, but they will want new ones in their places. And the arrangements which will have to be made, and which Lloyd George will undoubtedly have a large share in making, will lead to the establishment of an entirely new system which, while giving employers a wider field of labor and an immensely increased production, will, at the same time, provide working-men and women with greatly enlarged earning capacity, an earning capacity which will be largely based on their own energy, initiative, and persistence. A wide extension of what may be called co-operative payment by results may be looked for.

The good-will among classes introduced by the war will certainly help the changes. The net result to be looked for is a practical abolition of unemployment, the extension of the area of labor to great numbers of women, increased earning powers for individuals, and still more for the families as a whole, and a greater output of all kinds of products, not only manufactured articles, but also food products from the land. Accompanying all this will be higher profits for employers.

That this revolution can be accomplished in a day or even in a year is not to be expected. That it is the direction in which British social life is bound to trend cannot be doubted. I see Lloyd George as the engineer-in-chief of the whole operation. In conjunction with the new national land scheme the industrial reformation will provide a policy with a far-reaching scope and a practicability which will appeal to his long-sighted vision, his active mind, his scorn of past usages which litter the road of progress. That he will attempt to recreate the new social system on the wreckage of that which has been destroyed by the war I think is beyond all question.

But Lloyd George's future destiny is not confined to his work for his own race and nation. The war has lifted him to international prominence. He is now and will be henceforth the most-talked-of British statesman in all other civilized countries. He will still have enemies who will detest him, but no one in the future will attempt to deny his effectiveness. Respect will be accorded him by the statesmen of other nations and the democracy of other nations, the latter of whom will remember his lifelong fight for the poor. Such a man may well be of influence in determining not only the fate of his own people, but also the fate of the civilized community at large. I see approaching him, when this war is over, an opportunity far greater than anything fate has yet placed in his way. The world will be shuddering at the ghastliness of its recent experiences and asking if there is no way of guarding against the possibility of such a catastrophe in the years ahead. Among all the nations lately at war there will be but one desire— namely, the insuring of the enjoyment of peace for the generations to come. If that mood comes to exist, as it surely will, among all the nations when this present conflict is over, there are two men who, working together, may write their names indelibly on the history of the world. President Wilson's uplifting vision of an enduring peace by a mutually protective combination of nations is regarded by many as impracticable even as an illusion. I do not believe Lloyd George will regard it either as impracticable or as an illusion. His spirit will glow at the thought of it. The magnitude of the proposal will encourage him rather than check him. As to the difficulties in the way, he will tackle them with a confident smile. The tenacity and high-mindedness of President Wilson are qualities which will especially appeal to him. He will be able to supplement them with that ingenuity and practicalness which are an integral part of his genius for getting things done. I can see these two men, therefore, as collaborators in days not so very far ahead. In the collaboration Lloyd George will probably find his culminating task.

APPENDIX

MR. LLOYD GEORGE ON AMERICA AND THE EUROPEAN WAR

On the anniversary of President Lincoln's birthday, February 12, 1916, Mr. Lloyd George sent a remarkable message to the American people comparing the American Civil War with the European conflict. By the courtesy of the New York *Times* this message is presented here.

A LINCOLN DAY MESSAGE

I am very glad to respond to your request for a message for publication on Lincoln Day. I am glad because to my mind Abraham Lincoln has always been one of the very first of the world's statesmen, because I believe that the battle which we have been fighting is at bottom the same battle which your countrymen fought under Lincoln's leadership more than fifty years ago, and most of all, perhaps, because I desire to say how much I welcome the proof which the last few days have afforded that the American people are coming to realize this, too.

Lincoln's life was devoted to the cause of human freedom. From the day when he first recognized what slavery meant he bent all his energies to its eradication from American soil. Yet after years of patient effort he was driven to realize that it was not a mere question of abolishing slavery in the Southern States, but that bound up with it was a larger issue: That unless the Union abolished slavery, slavery would break up the Union.

Faced by this alternative, he did not shrink, after every other method had failed, from vindicating both Union and freedom by the terrible instrument of war. Nor after the die for war had been cast did he hesitate to call upon his countrymen to make sacrifice upon sacrifice, to submit to limitation upon limitation of their personal freedom, until, in his own words, there was a new birth of freedom in your land.

Is there not a strange similarity between this battle, which we are fighting here in Europe, and that which Lincoln fought? Has there not grown up in this continent a new form of slavery, a militarist slavery, which has not only been crushing out the freedom of the people under its control, but which in recent years has also been moving toward crushing out freedom and fraternity in all Europe as well?

Is it not true that it is to the militarist system of government which centers in Berlin that every open-minded man who is familiar with past history would point as being the ultimate source of all the expansion of armaments, of all the international unrest, and of the failure of all movements toward co-operation and harmony among nations during the last twenty years?

We were reluctant, and many of us refused to believe that any sane rulers would deliberately drench Europe in its own blood, so we did not face the facts until it was almost too late. It was not until August, 1914, that it became clear to us, as it became clear to Lincoln in 1861, that the issue was not to be settled by pacific means, and that either the machine which controlled the destinies of Germany would destroy the liberty of Europe or the people of Europe must defeat its purpose and its prestige by the supreme sacrifice of war. It was the ultimatum to Serbia and the ruthless attack upon Belgium and France which followed because the nations of Europe would not tolerate the obliteration of the independence of a free people without conference and by the sword, which revealed to us all the implacable nature of the struggle which lay before us.

It has been difficult for a nation separated from Europe by three thousand miles of sea and without political connections with its peoples, to appreciate fully what was at stake in the war. In your Civil War many of our ancestors were blind. Lord Russell hinted at an early peace. Even Gladstone declared "we have no faith in the propagation of free institutions at the point of the sword." It was left for John Bright, that man of all others who most loved peace and hated war, to testify that when our statesmen "were hostile or coldly neutral the British people clung to freedom with an unfaltering trust." But I think that America now sees that it is human unity and freedom which are again being fought for in this war.

The American people under Lincoln fought not a war of conquest, but a war of liberation. We to-day are fighting not a war of conquest, but a war of liberation—a liberation not of ourselves alone, but of all the world, from that body of barbarous doctrine and inhuman practice which has estranged nations, has held back the unity and progress of the world, and which has stood revealed in all its deadly iniquity in the course of this war.

In such wars for liberty there can be no compromise. They are either won or lost. In your case it was freedom and unity or slavery and separation, in our case military power, tyrannously used, will have succeeded in tearing up treaties and trampling on the rights of others, or liberty and public right will have prevailed. Therefore, we believe that the war must be fought out to a finish, for on such an issue there can be no such thing as a drawn war.

In holding this conviction, we have been inspired and strengthened beyond measure by the example and the words of your great President. Once the conflict had been joined, he did not shrink from bloodshed. I have often been struck at the growth of both tenderness and stern determination in the face of Lincoln, as shown in his photographs, as the war went on.

Despite his abhorrence of all that was entailed, he persisted in it because he knew that he was sparing life by losing it, that if he agreed to compromise, the blood that had been shed on a hundred fields would have been shed in vain, that the task of creating a united nation of free men would only have to be undertaken at even greater cost at some later day. It would, indeed, be impossible to state our faith more clearly than Lincoln stated it himself at the end of 1864.

"On careful consideration," he said, "of all the evidence it seems to me that no attempt at negotiation with the insurgent leader could result in any good. He would accept nothing short of severance of the Union, precisely what we will not and cannot give. His declarations to this effect are explicit and oft repeated.

He does not deceive us. He affords us no excuse to deceive ourselves; . . . between him and us the issue is distinct, simple, and inflexible. It is an issue which can only be tried by war and decided by victory."

That was the judgment of the greatest statesman of the nineteenth century during the last great war for human liberty. It is the judgment of this nation and of its fellow-nations overseas to-day.

"Our armies," said Lincoln, "are ministers of good, not evil." So do we believe. And through all the carnage and suffering and conflicting motives of the Civil War, Lincoln held steadfastly to the belief that it was the freedom of the people to govern themselves which was the fundamental issue at stake. So do we to-day. For when the people of central Europe accept the peace which is offered them by the Allies, not only will the allied peoples be free, as they have never been free before, but the German people, too, will find that in losing their dream of an empire over others, they have found self-government for themselves.

D. LLOYD GEORGE.

THE END

Lightning Source UK Ltd.
Milton Keynes UK
UKOW04f1949081117

312397UK00002B/252/P